New Age Yoga: 7 Paths of Awakening
© 2020 Authored, Edited and Self-published by Veren Riki Warren
www.bodyweightgurus.com / Instagram: @rix.official
Page design: Simona Marini, www.simonamarini.com / @simonamarini

I dedicate this book to my loving mother Shila Warren, who in giving me this life precedes any words that I can say.

Just as importantly, I dedicate this book to any and every being, consciousness and vibration. I offer this perspective in the hope that it will open your mind by enhancing your life and perception in some form or another. I hope you will hear my real voice in it, and the deep universal love that it is written with.

Peace and light, Hari Om ॐ

With special thanks to all of my Gurus, Teachers, Friends and Students, without whom I could not have written this book. You know who you are.

PREFACE

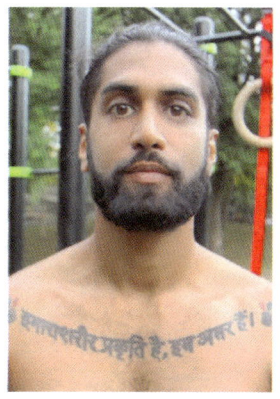

"The human body is the most complicated and intelligent machine that we know of. It is Nature's finest evolutionary development to date. When you were born, nobody gave you a manual for how to use it though - yet we must learn this in order to uncover our full potential if we are to get the most out of the life we have. I've dedicated my life to the study of this, because the body learns through practice and gives a man superpowers, and the mind learns through knowledge, giving him the wisdom of how to use it." – **Veren Riki Warren**

When I had decided to write this book, it was a daunting process at first – unravelling and putting down onto paper a myriad of memories and information accumulated over decades, boiling over inside and ready to burst out. I also decided that I didn't want to write a huge amount about myself since this is not an autobiography, this book is meant for sharing knowledge and not for singing my praises - yet I realised midway through writing that I have to give you some context to who I am and what experiences I've had in order to present this information to you. So here is a short introduction to that effect.

My full name is Veren Riki Warren. For the longest time I have pandered to the Westernisation of my name and used the altered version of "Ricky", but in this book I use my full and original Indian name to assert its origin. My mother named me Veren based on my Vedic astrological chart, as is the custom for naming Indian babies, and Riki as a middle name because she also liked that name.

The ancient language of India is known as *Sanskrit*. Every letter in the Sanskrit language system denotes a sound and meaning. The letter V denotes strength. The root *Veer-* in Sanksrit means "Warrior", or "Hero" depending on the context used, for example *Veerabhadra* (the black warrior avatar of Shiva and Warrior pose in Yoga), or *Veerasana* (Hero posture in Yoga). Shiva is commonly known as the Hindu deity of destruction, not in an anarchical way but in the sense of dissolution and transformation. All of his avatars and involvements in folklore have been that of a warrior's or teacher's nature. Hinduism is very nuanced and philosophical, its stories require a high level of self-inquiry and detachment from the limiting nature of ego to understand at depth.

It was therefore interesting for me to also find out more recently that my mother was born on the day of Shivratri, which is Shiva's birthday. What makes this even more coincidental is that I was born a week or so after the Hindu observation of Hanuman Jayanti, which is the birthday of Shiva's 11th incarnation Lord Hanuman. Hanuman became a close and loved warrior-devotee to Lord Rama who was a famous ancient king of India. Hanuman used a *Vajra* (mace) in battle, and his 'spiritual father' was *Vayu*, the Hindu God of Wind. They have a phrase in India which is *Naamasya Lakshanah*, roughly translated as "your name brings certain qualities in you"…

My mother often told me of how I was running at just 9 months old. An easily distracted and high energy child, my teachers found it hard to contain me or reign me in – I was sometimes given detentions for misbehaving and my reports would usually say something along the lines of "very intelligent, if he would only just focus and pay attention he would do very well".

I had my first meditative experience at 4 years old. It was at my grandparent's house, which when not overrun with my 16 cousins was a very quiet place. They had a TV but it was rarely on during the day. They would just sit in silence, perhaps reading, cooking or relaxing. Being in that environment does incredible things for one's mind. It creates a vacuum of sound, where the senses become enhanced to any changes in the environment. My grandmother Vimla (who incidentally helped to raise me with my single mother) had placed deities on top of an electric fireplace in the living room, which I used to sit in front of. I would stare at the flames flickering, and fell in absolute love with the sensation of the heat emerging. I would sit or lay there for an hour sometimes. I distinctly remember a few times, where I had zoned out from the warmth penetrating deep into my skin and muscles, and I began to feel shivers going up my spine and encasing my head. It felt the way it feels when you stretch first thing in bed in the morning, referred to as pandiculation.

This lead to the funny discovery that when I got these shivers I could feel the muscles around my ears and wiggle them! Hilariously I have retained this odd skill even to today. I would not say that this experience was enlightening at all (to my knowledge), but it became a meditative experience for me without even knowing what I was doing, which I would do every time I went to that house because I enjoyed how it made me feel. Warm, safe, still and peaceful. After all I was just a 4 year old child with a lot of energy, but had found something which could finally make me sit still.

My parents took me to learn martial arts from the young and impressionable age of 7 where I believe I developed much of my foundations for the things I have done as an adult. After a troubled childhood and teenage years, I got myself together enough to go on to higher education, eventually receiving a Batchelor's degree in Biology with Science Communication from Royal Holloway, University of London thanks to the encouragement, support and guidance of my family.

Today I have 28 years of multi-disciplinary training experience and 10 years of coaching as a result of this. My proudest achievements are;

- being the inventor of the *Iron Lotus* position (established 2015), a mixture of the jewel of Olympic rings *Iron Cross* and the jewel of yoga postures *Padmasana*, or *full Lotus*
- holding a current Guinness World Record for L-sit Muscle Ups on the Olympic rings (2019 - present)
- having qualified over 1000 personal trainers and therapists in my systems for teaching calisthenics, rehabilitation and mobility.
- being the first in the world to offer an industry accredited calisthenics instructor certification (2013)
- having become a fully qualified and leading biomechanics and movement coach/sports therapist
- competing or judging at international calisthenics competitions, also hosting the UK's first ever calisthenics competition in 2012
- presenting of lectures and workshops at conferences with thousands of attendees including the Health Optimisation Summit and the MeFitPro Summit.
- writing editorials and features for many major fitness publications including Men's Health and Men's Fitness, as well as other mainstream press and publications
- working history with some of the top global sporting brands including adidas, Under Armour, Reebok and more
- travelling and coaching innumerable coaches, athletes and members of the public across the globe including world champions of multiple sports in the UK, USA, Europe, India, Sri Lanka, Thailand, Bali and more.

Alongside this I feel I must mention over 20 years of study in science, world history, philosophy, theology, economics and many more fields. I'm a truth seeker, I feel like I was born to dig, climb and reach into obscurity for it. While your average Joe sits at home watching Netflix, I'm researching on my laptop and reading every night – I haven't had a TV set in my home since 2010.

Below is a diagram showing my 28 years of training in physical disciplines (excluding academics, music and other areas of study) – if you study it carefully, you will see that each and every discipline learnt had transferrable skills to offer to the next ones.. This is an important note for later on, when we discuss the accumulative effect of cross-discipline training and how this allows for faster learning, mimicking and understanding of technique.

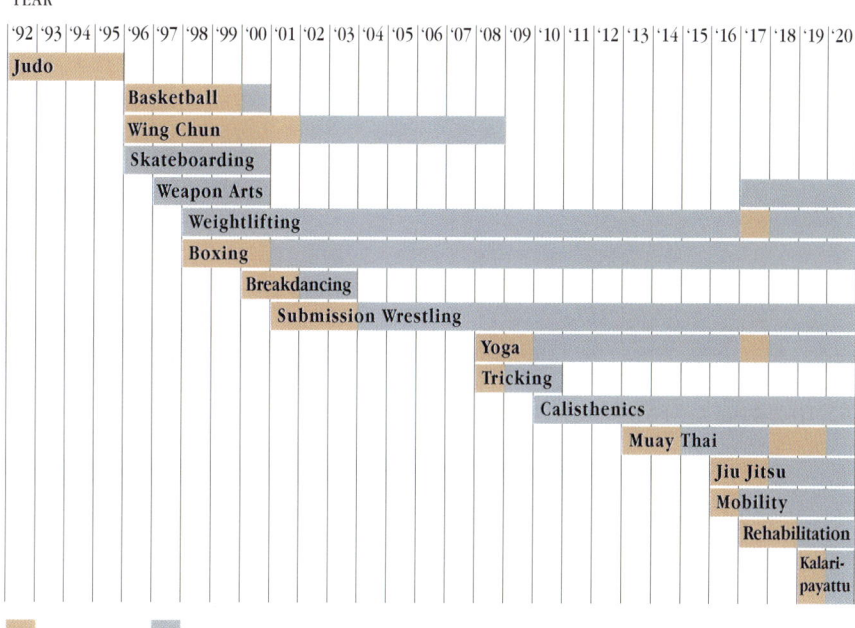

So this brings me to here and now. I got to the point 5 years ago in my coaching career where I was being told by my peers, clients, colleagues and pretty much anyone I shared my work with that I had enough quality and quantity of information/insights to offer that I should write a book on it all. I contemplated it and wanted to wait until I felt I had become someone who could authoritatively write something of that nature, and at long last I felt called, as if I was channelling information and being guided towards writing. It was time.

All knowledge has been given to us – there is nothing new under the sun. We are just, as they say in India, reliving our *karma*. That is to say, we are experiencing in cycles the accumulation of our energetic memory. Our ancestors live on in us and so does their knowledge, it is woven into the very fabric our being, our DNA. Anything that I can present to you in this book is not that of my discovery, but that of my intense study and arrangement. It is simply a detailed perception of multiple nuanced topics which I have tried to communicate and adapt to the principles of the modern era. To transform it all into a new form, more suitable for the minds of today. To be able to combine cross-disciplinary secrets and techniques into a more understandable and less disjointed set of cues, as well as being able to explain why you might want to do such things in the first place, without having to refer to blind faith. I wouldn't try to say I'm some kind of genius at all –it's only due to the learning of self-awareness, through simple dedication to the process of training and learning. The process is a beautiful thing – it makes great things happen without extra thinking needed, if you just follow the path and keep walking, you are sure to arrive.

Someone asked me what the purpose of this book is as I was writing it. I told them; "It's to put down into words an orderly compilation of information which has the potential to touch anyone in the world. This information can normally only be shared in such depth in person, over hours of conversation - but if I write it down, it can touch people I am not even in contact with, in their own time. They can absorb it as they want to, at their pace." See having met many influential people in my life I realised, in that moment when you meet someone for the first time and they ask you what you do, you don't usually have the opportunity to talk for hours. So a book is a great way to organise your thoughts and present them in a succinct way for people to digest alongside their normal life schedules. Bearing this in mind, I intentionally tried to keep this book short and concise so as to leave you yearning for more, since in that yearning is the awakening of self-inquiry, the fire which will take you forward.

If what you leave behind in the world is your legacy, then to be able to lay down and die one day knowing that I tried to leave the world a better place than when I got here is enough for me. I share this information because I believe there is something of value in it for each and every person, and I just want to share the joy and abilities that have arisen in me from this understanding and practice. They have changed my life, and today I hope you will read something which will change yours, for the better.

What this book is meant to be

- an introduction to a wide range of concepts, disciplines and fields of study from Eastern and Western culture
- a guide towards understanding your own nature and the collected wisdom around following certain paths
- an attempt to reason and make sense of a large volume of complex and nuanced information, for use in the modern era
- an introduction to both ancient India's wisdoms and the advanced research of modern science and technology, through my eyes
- a reference point for many concepts which you can research into further at your leisure

What this book is not meant to be

- absolute in its nature
- an attempt to consolidate every possible method of bettering oneself
- a dogma or politically aligned belief
- an overly detailed book on every topic mentioned
- intolerance or disproof of any other theories other than where specifically referred to and challenged

CONTENTS

CHAPTER 1: Western Science meets Eastern Wisdom............1

CHAPTER 2: The Composition of the Human Being............17

CHAPTER 3: Yogic Science, Concepts and Rituals............27

CHAPTER 4: Sport Science, Concepts and Programming............43

CHAPTER 5: New Age Yoga (7 Paths of Awakening)............59
- Breath Path..68
- Healing Path..73
- Movement Path..80
- Astral Path..85
- Scholar Path..90
- Rhythm Path..95
- Tantric Path..100

CHAPTER 6: Gurus, Coaches, Disciples and Students..........105

CHAPTER 7: Birth and Death..........117

CHAPTER 1

Western Science meets Eastern Wisdom

"I have not told you to believe it; I have not told you to disbelieve it. It is my experience, I am sharing it with you. You don't have to believe it, you don't have to disbelieve it. You have to inquire into it. You have to go to the same depths, to the same heights from where I am speaking, to the same centre of your being. Then you will understand it, not believe it. You will know it. Existence needs you, otherwise you wouldn't be here." – **Osho, I Celebrate Myself, Chapter 4**

First let us start by briefly examining the contexts of both modern science and ancient Indian Yogic philosophy. I'll be presenting information from published peer-reviewed journals, which is the most accepted form of modern science, alongside the traditional wisdom of the ancient Indian scriptures, which are where the philosophies of Yoga originated. So when we speak of the Yogic sciences we speak of those scriptures and teachings that were of Hindu origin, which means it's important to grasp some understanding of the principles behind this way of life. Hinduism is actually a relatively newer term compared to its ancient name, *Sanatana Dharma*. Sanatana Dharma is the 8-spoked *Wheel of Dharma*, or "duties of the righteous soul". It was designed to support the evolution of humanity on this earth and provide the entire population with spiritual guidance and objective morality, alongside knowledge of the dualistic principle of Sun-Moon. This was used not just in Hinduism but also in Jainism and Buddhism, having been translated later in the Far East to other concepts like *Bagua* and *Yin-Yang*. It stands proudly on the merits of its own truth, that there is an objective morality and that morals cannot be subjective. The intellect or logic cannot be the tool for moral reasoning, because while materialist and determinist views can reduce all of morality down to simple random mutations and natural selection, they cannot stitch together how those constructs arrived at moral reasoning.

The Wheel of Dharma

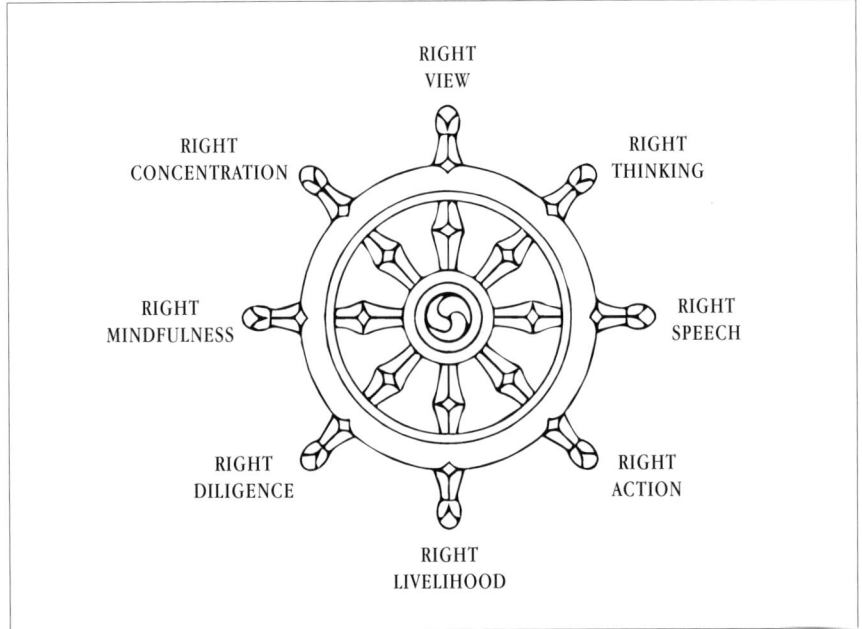

The term Hindu actually means a person of Himalayan Indus Valley genetic roots, the oldest known civilisation of the world who were also known as the Harappans. The Indus Valley Civilisation was a Bronze Age civilisation in the north-western regions of Bharat, which is now known as India. It was established from 3300 BCE to 1300 BCE, reaching its mature form from 2600 BCE to 1900 BCE. It is the oldest record of civilisation known to have existed in the entire world. When I say a civilisation, I mean the archaeological evidence of a large, expanding community with language, architecture, tools, medicine and so on.

The Indus River is one of the "Sapta Sindhu" (seven holy rivers), which have become very important pilgrimage points for people all over the world. The other six rivers considered as sacred are: the Ganges River, Yamuna River, Saraswati River, Godavari River, Narmada River and the

Kaveri River, which all originate in the ice capped Himalayas of northern India. The Harappan civilisation developed in the valley where the Indus River meets the Indian Ocean.

The Harrapans were indigenous to the Indian subcontinent, with a mix of Veddoid and Dravidian genetic ancestry. There was another group of indigenous Indians in the south called the Tamils, who are more "Dravidian" in their genetic ancestry, the Veddoids coming from northern genetic pools. These groups have intermingled and shared culture for thousands of years, such that all people of Indian ethnicity are now a mixture of both gene pools, as well as having some genetic remnants of historical cultural mixing with the Aryans (Indo-European), Sinoids (Mongoloid) and other populations.

So the word Hindu did not actually represent a religion, but was actually an exonym later coined by the Persians to identify the indigenous people who lived in the Indus Valley. This civilisation had a way of life which included a gigantic volume of information on the actual philosophies and logistics of running and maintaining a civilisation. The Hindu philosophy and theology incorporates such diverse views on the concept of God that it is truly adapt in encouraging the learner to use critical thinking to arrive at their own conclusion. Hinduism is so diverse that it has even been described by scholars as polytheism, monotheism, henotheism, panentheism, pantheism, monism, agnostic, humanism, atheism or non-theism, which is practically almost every type of belief you could possibly hold. Indeed India for this reason have never been about belief but about inquiry – Bharat has never in its history of 7000 years of civilisation banned or discourage the practice of any faith.

Paramahamsa Yogananda was a great Indian scholar and Yogi who was sent to the USA by his Guru to unite the deeper concepts of monotheism with the Vedas. He undertook this task to great effect in the early

1900's, where he had great success in reconnecting the dots between the Christian faith and Vedic wisdom. As I have already said all faiths are tolerated and in fact encouraged in India as a means of self-discovery, with Yoga being cited as a path towards self-realisation, often referred to by Yogananda as "India's Universal science of God-realization". The Bhagavad Gita for example, explains to a spiritual person of any faith how they might come closer to his or her faith through the processes of meditation, breath control and yoga. Therefore it is a timeless piece which is not meant to divide or separate believers from disbelievers – it simply attains to logic and discusses the metaphysical aspects of life and the universe in such a way that there is room for everyone to take something home from it.

For this book I want to focus on the vast knowledge and intelligence which came out of this region of the world and how it can benefit us, no matter where you are from or what you may believe. It spans a variety of genres, including but not limited to the *Vedas* (religious), *Upanishads* (philosophical), *Puranas* (folklore/legends), *Sutras and Sashtras* (fields of study and sciences). The Vedas are said to be *apaurusheya* (not of human agency) – the belief is that we were given this information from beings of higher states of consciousness. The others were all mostly written by saints, scholars and monks who had divine connection or intervention. When you read these works, some as old as 5000BCE, you can understand why these are thought to be divine in nature.

Some notable examples of these expansive texts and their fields of study include but are not limited to;

- *Vaimanika Shastra* (aeronautics)
- *Vastu Shastra* (architecture)
- *Surya Siddhanta* (astronomy)

- ***Artha Shastra*** (politics and economics)
- ***Bhautika Shastra*** (physics)
- ***Rasayana Shastra*** (chemistry)
- ***Jiva Shastra*** (biology)
- ***Shilpa Shastra*** (mechanics and sculpture)
- ***Natya Shastra*** (performing arts)
- ***Yoga Sutras*** (spiritual fulfilment)
- the famous ***Kama Sutra*** (sexual and emotional fulfilment)
- and saving the best until last, the ***Bhagavad Gita*** ("God's song"), which is referred to as "India's Universal Science of God Realization."

Although the Vedas, Puranas and Upanishads were philosophical and theological texts, their significance is perhaps even bigger as we are about to find out, since the latter Shastras and Sutras were inspired by and progressing on from the earlier Vedas. These bodies of texts are not only incredibly old and detailed but also often written in rhyme or poetically, adding to their magnificence. They detail entire methods for building language, society, music scales, physical disciplines of exercise and combat, dance, God realisation and more. They are works clearly aimed at connecting us to both our humanness and our inner-divinity (higher self).

As an example, the Bhagavad Gita (a section of a bigger text called the Mahabharata) by itself holds so much divine information – it is sung in rhyme with 700 verses. The entire text of the Mahabharata is over 100,000 stanzas, 15 times longer than the Bible and as long as Homer's Iliad and the Odyssey combined. Written in such a profound way, even the Dalai Lama said that when he is troubled he would read and meditate on one random line from the Gita to put his mind at ease. It is a text with such wisdom, even though it has been dated to over 5000 years ago (!) its meaning is still outside of our ability to fully comprehend. It is the same with advanced mathematical formulae – we can understand them to be true by calculation, but it takes many years of technological development before we can understand their actual applications in the real world. That's why they say surely it was not of human agency, but delivered by Lord Krishna on the battlefield to Arjuna.

Arjuna, a man leading an army to defend his people from attack, sees his father, his brother and his Guru on the opposite side. He is overwhelmed with emotion and tension, he cannot understand what he should do. Krishna delivers him the Bhagavad Gita in a back and forth Q&A style, while Arjuna asks him existential questions and Krishna answers with eloquence and grace. It is said that when Krishna delivered this, all of the Gods and even time itself stood still to hear the song of the universe put so eloquently. Let us examine some of the verses;

"Why do you worry without cause? Whom do you fear without reason? Who can kill you? The soul is neither born, nor does it die.

What did you lose that you cry about? What did you bring with you, which you think you have lost? What did you produce, which you think got destroyed?

You did not bring anything – whatever you have, you received from here. Whatever you have given, you have given only here. Whatever you took, you took from here. Whatever you gave, you gave back.

You came empty handed, you will leave empty handed. What is yours today, belonged to someone else yesterday, and will belong to someone else the day after tomorrow. You are mistakenly enjoying the thought that this is yours. It is this false happiness that is the cause of your sorrows. Change is the law of the universe.

What you think of as death, is indeed life. In one instance you can be a millionaire, and in the other instance you can be steeped in poverty. Yours and mine, big and small – erase these ideas from your mind. Then everything is yours and you belong to everyone.

This body is not yours, neither are you of the body. The body is made of fire, water, air, earth and ether, and will disappear into these elements. But the soul is permanent – so who are you?"

– Sri Krishna, excerpt from the Bhagavad Gita, 3000BCE

Millions of cells die each minute and millions take birth in our body. The body is stuck in transience, in a constant cycle of birth and rebirth. In juxtaposition, the Soul is on par with God. It is described as "infinite existence, consciousness and bliss." It is indestructible, inscrutable, immutable and permanent. The Soul is eternal, omnipresent, immovable, constant and everlasting. It is beyond birth and death.

These texts are so spectacular as to even contain facts which were at that time still undiscovered by science. For instance in the Hindu prayer/hymn Hanuman Chalisa written by the great Indian poet, philosopher and saint Shri Goswami Tulsidas (1532-1623), Hanuman was said to have leaped up at the sun thinking it to be a fruit, and tried to eat it. The text states;

Yug Sahastra Yojan Par Bhanu
Leeyo Taahi Madhur Phal Janu
"The Sun is at a distance of Yug Sahastra Yojan
He swallowed it thinking it was a sweet fruit"

According to the conversion as per Vedic Literature:

1 Yug = 12000
1 Sahastra = 1000
1 Yojan = 8 miles
Thus
12000 X 1000 X 8 = 96,000,000 miles
1 mile = 1.6 kms
96,000,000 * 1.6 kms = 153,600,000 kilometres

This is exactly the same approximation according to the latest findings of modern astronomy and science - we know that the earth's orbit around the sun is not a circle and is slightly elliptical therefore, the distance between the earth and the sun varies depending on the time it is calculated, but averages at 92,955,807 miles (149,597,870 km).
Tulsidas died in 1623. Not until 30 years later in 1653 did the scientific Astronomer Christiaan Huygens finally calculate the distance on behalf of science, using the phases of the planet Venus to arrive at the same conclusion. A brilliant example of where science could have been inspired to research the statements of the Vedas and arrived at the conclusion later.

One of the greatest texts on astronomical references is the *Surya Siddantha*, written in 600AD by Indian astronomer and polymath Varahamihira. The scripture states that the earth is of a spherical shape, at a time when it was considered heresy in Abrahamic religions to dispute that the Lord's Earth was not flat. Surya Siddantha makes several estimates, some simple examples are shown below;

- Earth's diameter at 8,000 miles (actual 7,928 miles)
- Moon's diameter at 2,400 miles (actual 2,160 miles)
- the distance between the moon and the earth to be 258,000 miles (now known to vary: 221,500–252,700).

The text is also known for some of the earliest known discussion of fractions and trigonometric functions in the entire world. Self-taught mathematician Srinivasa Ramanujan learnt advanced mathematic formulae from Surya Siddantha and other Vedic literature, which he sent forward in a manuscript to the world's leading mathematicians at the time including the famous G.H. Hardy of Cambridge University. Hardy's response to this manuscript was that these groundbreaking "new" theorems "defeated him completely". He remarked that he "had never seen anything in the least like them before". Another example of ancient Indian literature furthering the world of science and humanity, but never acknowledged due to the scientific fear of associating with a religious text. It can be said that if science fails to heed the guidelines of spirit that it will always simply be playing catch up.

If we look at science's most recent explanations of how life and humans came to be, we can see that it has simply rediscovered truths which have already been indicated. The *Vishnu Purana* states:

"Now, dear Brahma, create duly nether worlds, earth, rivers, seas and forests in the Cosmic Sphere. The following too should be created: trees, mountains, bipeds, animals, birds, Gandharvas, Siddhas, Yakshas, Rakshasas, beasts of prey and all those living beings of **eight million and four hundred thousand species**. *They are to be of four different types, each consisting of two million and one hundred thousand species.*

They are:
(1) Udbhijjas or species of vegetation that grow breaking up the surface of the earth;
(2) Svedajas or sweat-born ones such as insects, worms etc.;
(3) Jarayujas (viviparous beings) and
(4) Andajas (oviparous beings). You create all these things quickly."

Again, nobody is asking you to believe that this conversation between the deities Vishnu and Brahma actually happened. But the information contained within is of utmost curiosity, since modern science also estimates the total number of species on Earth at approx. 8.7 million, extraordinarily close to the 8.4 million mentioned in this stanza from 1000BC. Furthermore, the Purana states that a human must pass through 8.4 million karmic rebirths, from a single celled protozoan all the way through evolution before they gain the competence to handle a human body, which is the most complicated individual bio-system on the planet. This revelation does not conflict with the famous Darwin and his book on evolutionary theory, *On The Origin of Species (1859)*. It was however, written almost 3000 years earlier.

This is why it is said that this life is a gift – it is a chance to use and experience the most intelligent and self-aware technology that is the human being, Nature's finest creation in all its billions of years of evolution. I mention these specific references in an effort to create space for the understanding that just because something is ancient or has religious connotations, it does not destroy the validity of the information even from a modern perspective. Information is information, regardless of the deeper beliefs of a person about how the information might have come to be. And those sources should be respected and given a chance considering their enormous contributions through history to math, science, art and many more fields of study which help us as humans to get closer to understanding our universe and thus ourselves. There will be much more on the revelations from these texts as we move forward into discussing the use of this information in the attainment of that goal.

We don't talk about any fictional characters or archetypes from Hollywood as being real, but the lessons from their stories definitely hit hard culturally, which is why and more importantly how we identify and empathise with them, on occasion taking specific characters as inspirations for our own actions and life. Imagine the people of the year 3000, laughing and thinking that we must have "believed in" the cartoon characters of the Looney Tunes - it doesn't matter if they and their stories were real or not, what matters is what was said about them and what can be learnt from their characters. How we apply that understanding to give life meaning is the intrinsic and real value of all learning.

Now when we speak about modern science, I am referring to the most commonly held beliefs about what has been calculated or measured, peer-reviewed and published as "accepted science". For me to debate with scientists around the ins and outs of these is impossible, since I will cover so many fields of study I can only go on what is currently accepted as the latest and mainstream understanding in science – and this is because science is constantly undergoing change as it develops and finds deeper expression of the ultimate truth.

In the Western world, the Greeks were heralded as the bringers of knowledge and science. The Greeks brought about a huge enlightenment especially during the renaissance, their scientists also believing in the Gods of Zeus, Apollo, Hades, Poseidon and more. The first of the Greeks to make the distinction between animate and inanimate matter was Aristotle, who asserted that it was a major problem in philosophy. He wrote the laws of physics as a way to explain the phenomena of inanimate matter (the material world), and the study of metaphysics to attempt answering questions of an existential nature.

Eventually through scientific enquiry we found the atom, and believed it to be the smallest thing in the universe - not until we discovered protons, neutrons, quarks and bosons did we realise the ever increasing micro- and macro-natures of the universe. When quarks are observed they are seen to appear and disappear out of existence, which came as a huge surprise to scientists who once believed that this was the only reality in existence.

The fact that an object of mass can spontaneously and randomly come in and out of this reality in itself proves the existence of other dimensions – it has to have come from somewhere!

The latest understanding on this is that alternative realities and dimensions do therefore exist. We can actually mathematically and geometrically calculate and agree upon the existence of multiple dimensions (currently it is believed that there are 10, according to String Theory). A dimension is classified as a plane of space and/or consciousness, where all sentient and non-sentient beings are limited within the plane they reside in, using their senses to interpret the perceivable world around them. Here is a simple way of understanding dimensions theory with some illustrations.

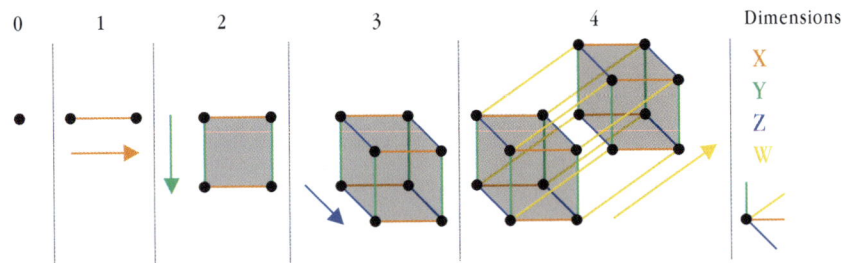

Here we can see geometry being used to illustrate the concepts of dimensions. The first three dimensions are the x, y and z axes which give us height, length and width. The fourth dimension is purported to be the axis that the 3D object moves along, so the fourth axis is **time**. However, time is not a physical plane or dimension – it is a perceived one. Time's effects can be observed, but it cannot be held, it has no physical dimensions. From this we can understand two things:

> 1. That beings cannot completely perceive or observe other dimensions above them. They can only reason (philosophise) to

them existing or not. If you were to touch a piece of paper with your finger, a 1D or 2D being living on the paper would not be able to perceive the height of your finger, because height is information that exists in the 3rd dimension, an axis they have no perception of. That being would just see a slivery line of your finger. If you push this finger through the paper, the being would then see a line of your nail or knuckle. It would appear to a 1D or 2D being that you are shapeshifting, because you are appearing in and out of their dimensional reality in different shapes and colours. To those beings, you would be considered a God, maybe.

So if consciousness or beings exist in higher dimensions or planes of existence such as the 5D or 6D, they could come in and out of our 3D world which is moving along the 4D of time, and we would observe them as shapeshifters or God-like due to their "powers".

2. Secondly, it infers that there are things in existence that we cannot comprehend due to the limited nature of our ability to sense and perceive. But we have been gifted with intelligence like no other – the intelligence to logic and reason our way to the truth. The only issue is, look how long it's taken us as a human race to even get here with this much information, and we are still not really any closer to understanding it all that much. Information exists on Google sure, but this doesn't mean people are intelligent – in fact the advent of the internet has lead to a rise in "Google experts" who believe they are intelligent because they have all that knowledge to hand on a phone. But if all technology ceased to exist tomorrow, you would see the real intelligence of the average human to even survive.

And if surviving is not intelligence, then what even is intelligence? A commodity for showing off at that point, but without real value. It is akin to having a book of advanced, complex maths formulas but not having the slightest clue about what they're actually used for. Intelligence is not just memory. It is the application of memory.

Application of memory requires joining bits of information together through a higher level of perception than just recall or math. It requires a robust, fast, well learned and experienced machine. It is educating and then understanding we need for our evolution, not artificial intelligence. Because it is exactly that, not just physically but philosophically. It's artificial in its very nature, pseudo-intelligence/without life to it. Calculation alone does not equal rationality of thinking. *"An eye for an eye makes the whole world blind"*, as Gandhi said. Intuitiveness, an ability of our regal soul, is not available to the robot, who much like the primitive animal simply reacts and responds without prior moral insight.

It is exactly our humanness that makes us above the robot in nature. There are some people recently like Elon Musk who say that bio-robotics is the way forward for evolving the human mind and body. That we should merge with machines because AI is threatening to be too widespread and make us incompetent. All sounds a bit Skynet to me. Musk asserts that the only restriction to this happening now is that we cannot merge the brain with the internet properly due to low bandwidth of data transfer. Essentially he's saying that the brain can't tap into machine intelligence yet because it can't access the information quickly enough from "the cloud". The technologist's proposal is that they add a new layer to the brain! Now listen what I'm trying to ask you is why do we need to get as complex as adding new layers into the brain, when we only use some 8% of it as it is? It is this exact underestimation of the human being and overestimation of technology which is leading us into these kinds of projects and away from reclaiming our innate human powers.

The human being is already the most sophisticated and intelligent technology we know of. So why not evolve this one to its maximum capability, before we even look at the risks, costs and equal opportunities around adding new bits? I am all for progress but completely against dehumanisation, because being **human** (not just book-smart) is exactly what separates us from everything else and makes us the most spiritually capable beings on this planet.

We are now in an era where we are not just losing our spirituality but so dependent on technology and convenience that we've become immobile - we are actually regressing in terms of ability both physically and spiritually. Immobilisation has become one of the leading causes of injury and pain in the 21st century. If we want to evolve to Homo sapiens 2.0, I hold that we should do it through becoming fully fledged, self-engineered beings without the use of unnecessary and quite frankly unnatural adaptations such as genetic manipulation and robotics.

There have been many alternative methods over the ages for us to come to understand how to improve self-awareness, intelligence and performance, without the need for such overdrawn explanations and technology. We shall delve into these as we move on, these particular methods being more an ingenious matter of process, rather than reasoning. They can show you how to gain real power - not through showing off abilities or technologies, but through the realisation of self which occurs alongside practice. The body will inevitably perish, but consciousness is always expanding.

CHAPTER 2

The Composition of the Human Being

The Indian philosopher and mystic Sadhguru (Jaggi Vasudev) once said that human beings can do magical things – we can turn an apple into a human being, our body has the necessary intelligence and technology in it to do such an amazing piece of work. Or as Arthur C. Clarke once said,

"Magic is just a science that we don't understand yet."

Now without making this too technical, I will do my best to give a brief but concise summary of the human body from a scientific, biological perspective. There are 11 major systems in the human organism, which are the integumentary, skeletal, muscular, nervous, endocrine, cardiovascular, lymphatic, respiratory, digestive, urinary, and reproductive systems. Each has its own detailed anatomy map and is considered separate for study although obviously they work holistically together (at least when functioning well). Optimising, maintaining and healing those has been a focus of the entire world medical community for millennia.

A type of connective tissue known as fascia has been now researched more deeply by leading sport scientists and is being called "the structural organ", which has a different anatomy chart from the other structural systems such as the muscular, skeletal and integumentary (skin, nails, hair). This fascia acts as a webbing, permeating through the entire body and touching pretty much every strand of tissue, fibre of muscle and inch of bone throughout. In effect, it connects the other "connective tissues" together.

Scientist and writer of "Anatomy Trains" Thomas Myers was the most prominent figure in mapping out this fascial system and assessing its role in the body. At the time most scientists would use cross-section when they were dissecting bodies for examination – this means they would cut through an arm and look at the layers all at once. What Myers did was to simply peel the layers off one by one, systematically exposing each layer of tissue for examination across the whole body. What he found is still creating ripples in anatomy science today – the fascia, a clear, elastic material was able to connect tension originating in one part of the body like the neck to another location, sometimes all the way down to the foot. He mapped out these lines of fascia which hold elastic tension and are capable of learning memory. The ramifications for the study of human biomechanics and movement were huge – our understanding of how the body actually works mechanically would be changed forever.

Myers also wrote in his book about a concept called bio-tensegrity. The idea is that the human body does not hold posture or position by stacking the bones, but by a complex set of tensioned strings which formed in particular patterns across the body – enter the fascia. Myers made models of the spine, leg, hips and more to demonstrate that bio-tensegrity was the mechanical means of postural tension and so "structure" in the human body.

The term tensegrity was founded by American architect Buckminster Fuller in the 1960's, who asserted the following:

"Tensegrity, tensional integrity or floating compression is a structural principle based on a system of isolated components under compression inside a network of continuous tension, arranged in such a way that the compressed members (usually bars or struts) do not touch each other, while the pre-stressed tensioned members (usually cables or tendons) delineate the system spatially."

Translation: A structure of dense components connected by and held up via a perfect balance of tension across strings, where none of the parts touch each other, creating space inside and through.

So what Myers did was to apply that principle to the body, in the process demonstrating how we move in set patterns and why some movements are more biomechanically favourable than others regardless of individual muscle contribution. More on this later.

Now this fascial system physically connects in with all the other systems – one of those that it has a deep connection with is the nervous system, which is what actually controls where tension is held and where it is not, by means of sending or stopping signals to and from the brain regarding the voluntarily contraction or relaxation of tissues. These messages are sent via a type of neuron called a motor path (signalling paths for muscle fibre contraction).

The nervous system can be divided into two parts, the Parasympathetic (PSNS) and Sympathetic (SNS) nervous systems. The PSNS is responsible for your resting and healing activities, and the SNS for your conscious, active response to sense stimuli. Within the SNS, there are voluntary actions and involuntary actions. Voluntary actions are of course, voluntary contractions. Involuntary actions are called reflexes. The last 10 years of sport science has made astonishing progress in understanding the role of reflexes in the body and how we can "hack" them with the rest of our nervous system for training purposes.

The body has reactions built into it for protection, for example the Stretch reflex, which protects the muscles from tearing when lengthening, or the Knee-Jerk reflex, which protects the tendons from damage. It also holds tension lodged deep in both the conscious and subconscious mind, expressed as contraction signals – otherwise known as the emotional and physical trauma held in your body from previous incidents, injuries, accidents and fears. This tension left in the body causes dysfunction on all levels of our health including emotional, physical, mental and spiritual. Therefore these techniques are of extreme importance in the healing and progressive development of the body.

What's more, there is now increasing evidence to suggest that our organs, such as those of the digestive system, the stomach and intestines, have their own brain. Or said in a different way, their own autonomous control centres which can also communicate with the brain. These organs also hold host to such a volume of friendly-bacteria (pre/probiotics) that they are actually a mini-ecosystem, or a microcosm in themselves. Their environment is our body, and they live with us symbiotically by helping us to break down our food, getting their food and home in the process. We actually have more bacterial cells in our body than we do human cells – now that is food for thought. So what is actually driving all these cells and processes?

The Hidden 12th Biological System

> *"All matter is merely energy condensed to a slow vibration."*
> **– Bill Hicks, American Comedian**

Don't let Hicks' job fool you – comedy is an ingenious way to weave the substance of reality into a joyful perspective.

There is another system that has been mapped out which every human has, but for reasons of not being able to observe or dissect it, is not taught in modern western science – it is the Bio-electro-magnetic system. Although it cannot be observed with the eyes as such, it can be measured with the use of tools. The heart for example, emits an electromagnetic pulse which can be detected up to 12 feet away from the body, by standard medical equipment. As such, the Yogic philosophy maintains that so do all of the organs and the entire cellular network.

Bio- meaning life, and electro-magnetic meaning the conjoined forces of electricity and magnetism working together to create moving energy with magnetic charge (+/− polarity). This energy is referred to in the Hindu Yogic science as *prana*, in the Chinese Buddhist system as *chi*, the Japanese Buddhist system as *kii* and the Western metaphysical sciences as ether, orgone or zero-point energy (proved by the likes of Nikola Tesla and William Reich). The routes along which this energy travels through the body are called *nadis* (Yogic) or *meridians* (Chinese), and the "gates" or "vortex" like meeting points are referred to as *chakras* by all. It is said that this is the fundamental, underpinning system of the entire human body, and that even though dis-ease and dysfunction can be worked on at several levels, if worked on at this level it will directly lead to the repair of the physically manifested systems, which are after all simply held together by the electromagnetic forces and energies which form our energy body, or "light body". According to Dr. Reich, orgone is scientifically measured and found in high amounts in more alive, natural settings and living food sources (plants are alive when you eat them). He claims that it is this source of energy that is absolute healing for our bodies.

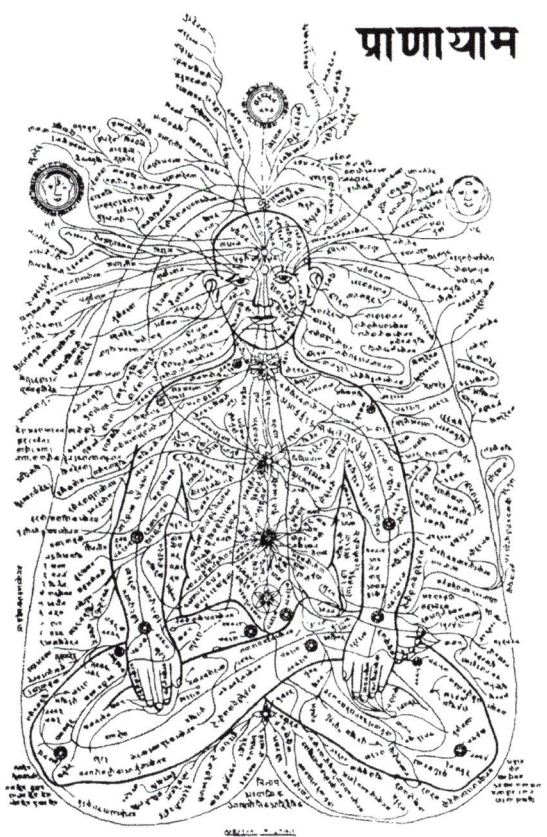

"Gross man seldom or never realises that his body is a kingdom, governed by Emperor Soul on the throne of the cranium, with subsidiary regions in their six spinal centers or spheres of consciousness (medullary, cervical, dorsal, lumbar, sacral and coccygeal). This theocracy extends to over a throng of obedient subjects – 27,000 billion cells endowed with sure if seemingly automatic intelligence by which they perform all duties of bodily growth, transformations and dissolutions, and 50 million substratal thoughts, emotions and variations of alternating phases in man's consciousness, over an average lifetime of 60 years."

– Paramahansa Yogananda, Autobiography of a Yogi

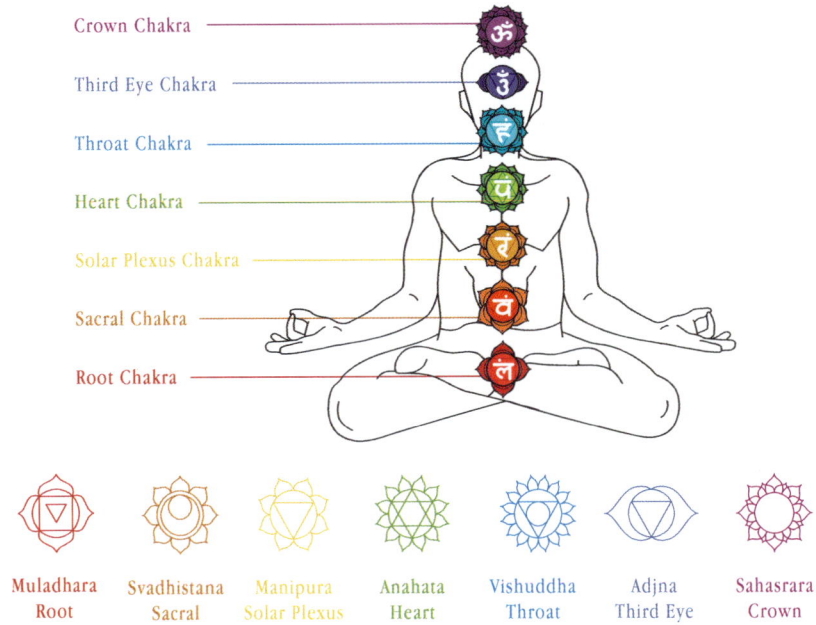

The 12-petalled heart chakra *Anahata* for example, means "unstruck" or "that which cannot be struck, injured or killed", meaning that the soul, residing in the heart chakra, is invincible. According to the Yogic science there are 114 chakras, each representing a different dimension of life and perception. It is said that 2 are outside and above the body, with 4 automatically activated by means of basic survival. The other 108 represent levels of perception and experience which we can open up through certain practices.

In the Yogic texts, Shiva was said to have given us this information having arrived on Earth some 7000 years ago as the avatar *Adiyogi*, the first Yogi. His origin unknown, his name even, unknown. But his legend has echoed through the ages, and still the name is known all over the world. Shiva, according to Sadhguru, means "That which is not" in Sanskrit. Shi-Va. That is what the force he represents is called. The nothingness, the immense inert energy held by stillness. Shiva is often called the God of destruction, but many scholars agree it to be more accurate to call him the God of transformation, of purification and growth, since all of these depend on the destruction of a previous condition, so a new and better state can arise.

In this form as Adiyogi, Shiva experimented with his human avatar and formulated 108 methods or processes by which these chakras or energy vortexes could be activated. During this period of experimentation on Mount Kailash in the Tibetan Himalayas, people came to observe this man who was either uncontrollably dancing in ecstacy or seated in absolute silent meditation. Eventually, these 108 methods were taught to a group of humans named the Saptarishis (7 disciples), who had gathered around him and did years of meditation in awe of him before he finally revealed this information to them. Shiva then instructed the Saptarishis to go forth and spread these methods to the world, for the benefit and sake of all humanity – this is where the many different styles of yoga and meditation that we have today are said to have originated. Many of these processes are detailed in the Sutras, Shastras, Upanishads and Vedas as mentioned at the beginning of this book. One of the most notable of these 7 Rishis, known as Agastyamuni, followed Shiva's instructions with the most vigour. Agastyamuni was the great Vedic sage who walked south and spread the Yogic sciences of Shiva across all of India, right to the bottom tip. He is still, alongside countless other real men, documented in history and revered today.

The number 108 has significant meaning, especially if one considers the fact that it is a full cycle of the number 9 in the times table. Expressions of 9 in the building of the universe's patterns, also known as the Sigma Code, was known to the Freemasons, Nikola Tesla, Leonardo di Vinci, the ancient Egyptians, the ancient Yogis and many more. 108 appears as the number of beads on a mala or full set of prayer beads as well as the number of openable chakras, according to Yogic science. It is considered a holy number of creation in cycles. Standard degrees of bisection through a circle always equal 9 if you add their numbers to each other, for instance 360, 270, 180, 90, 45 and so on. Using this model of 9 in geometry you can either draw lines through it to make angles, or draw polygons within it to make shapes. When you look at the patterns of 9 you can visually understand the concepts of the singularity and the vacuum.

Inward divergence (bisections at degrees of 9): Singularity

Outward divergence (polygons with corner angles of 9): Vacuum

A final note for this chapter is to touch on the topic of consciousness and the subconscious mind. Modern science has come relatively far enough to agree upon the existence of other dimensions, yet still not so far as to accept the bio-electromagnetic or chakra system as a legitimate system of the body worth mapping and studying. This is where the ancient wisdom of the Yogic sciences have shed light on our ignorance.

The conscious mind is said to be operating only during *alpha* (α) and *beta* (β) brain waves, alpha being "on autopilot" and beta being intense focus or concentration. The subconscious mind is operating under *theta* (θ) and *delta* (δ) brain waves - theta being the dream-state and delta being deep sleep. It is now known that during theta brain wave state the subconscious mind downloads and stores information from the conscious mind. The only time that this happens in adults is when we are falling asleep or waking up, so a small window like this can be used to listen to affirmations or to retain information we need to learn and recall longer term. Think of the language learning audiobooks that claim you can listen when you sleep and learn. Well technically they were correct, if only for an hour or two before you go into deep sleep.

It comes as no surprise really that children are actually in the state of theta during all of their waking hours until around the age of 7, demonstrating just how impressionable they are. It is interesting to note that after 7 the human brain develops a stronger sense of ego and superego, i.e. what do I think of myself, and what do others think of me? Before that, they are mostly in a dream state of exploration, a more natural state of being at one with nature. Therefore the time in a child's life when they are between 3 and 7 are where they are most impressionable and learning their fundamental schema for the world (after imprints given at birth and onwards). The deep sleep state of delta brain waves is where the consciousness has fully disconnected from the body, or as Parahamsa Yogananda says in his book Autobiography of a Yogi;

"The rejuvenating effects of sleep are due to man's temporary unawareness of body and breathing. The sleeping man becomes a yogi. Each night he unconsciously performs the yogic Rite of releasing himself from bodily identification and merges the prana (life force) with healing currents in the main brain region and in the 6 sub dynamos of his spinal centers (6 main bodily chakras, Muladhara through to Ajna). Unknowingly the sleeper is thus recharged by the cosmic energy that sustains all life."

CHAPTER 3
Yogic Science, Concepts and Rituals

योगश्चित्तवृत्तिनिरोधः ॥२॥

Yogaś Citta-Vṛtti-nirodhaḥ

"Yoga is mind-fluctuation-restraint"

– Patanjali's Yoga Sutras 1.2

The word Yoga has come to mean many things across the world, most recently conjuring up images of everything from enlightened meditating saints to flamboyant contortion artists. Yoga is popularly understood in the West today to be a largely physical practice, however the practicing of postures is of much less relevance to the true goal of yoga in the Hindu tradition. This is why we cannot separate or isolate the practice of Yoga from the culture it was created and propagated in.

The word *Yoga* (Sanskrit योग) is derived from the root *Yuj* (युज्) "to attach, join, harness, yoke". In context it is essentially spoken of as a state of "Union" with the supreme Godhead, or highest source of consciousness. There are two main types of yoga. *Hatha* and *Raja*. Hatha Yoga is principled in *Nadi Shuddi* – cleansing of the energetic pathways/channels of the body through the daily performance of bodily rituals. In Raja Yoga the principle aim is to achieve *Samadhi*, or bliss state. What the majority of the world are calling Yoga nowadays is mostly the practice of the Hatha style *asana* (postures) but with faster and more varied sequences, which has led to the creation of the Western-influenced style of *Vinyasa*. Vinyasa Yoga has unfortunately now become a more compartmentalised system of Yoga since it does not offer the full depth of cross-disciplinary work which is needed to fulfil union with the higher nature, the original goal of Yoga as Union. Vinyasa is mostly based in being a physical, practical system, with much of the deeper meaning lost on its students who do not enquire into the philosophy of its true nature.

This is not to say that the other elements are not taught at all, but not with enough consistency, accountability and balance of practice. It also doesn't mean that there's no benefit to the more asana focused practice of Yoga – it has immense and innumerable benefits for the health, strength, skill and vitality of the body, thus helping to maintain this vehicle fit for the command of the mind's true expression and manifestation. I'm just saying that if a science is adapted into various methods, the core structure and purpose of it cannot change or it ceases to be the science that it was called – Yoga, meaning Union. Union with the eternal part of us that does not die, or the *atma*, the soul.

Anything else which is created and aspires to the same goal would be intelligent to take into account the whole system, not just one route. Sure, a select few may reach the goal through asana with pure talent and dedication. But the majority of people that yoga is taught to could be given more guidance and access to the other aspects of yoga including breath work, meditation and self-study. Otherwise, and I say this without judgement, you could say a class that is based purely on asana without the teaching of consciousness, is simply the unconscious practice of postures.

Patanjali asserts that you must experience the individual soul, because recognising the fragment of the Godhead inside you brings such bliss that you will want to be in it forever – this is the experience of Samadhi. It is the duty of every human being to try and explore what is there within themselves. Our thoughts and senses are always directed outwards, but if we look inwards to visualise, we can see and have a vision of the soul that exists inside our own body. Other yogis have gone further to say that if you want to experience this at the fullest depth, you must make your body into a proper place (a temple) for the Supreme Being to actually reside in. The Supreme Being or Godhead is associated with so much bliss that it is not comparable to the bliss of the individual soul.

The *Yoga Sūtras* (approx. 200BCE) are the collection of 196 Sanskrit sutras (aphorisms) on the theory and practice of yoga compiled by the Indian sage Patanjali, who curated knowledge and practices tied to Yoga from a vast array of Vedic texts and scriptures. The Yoga Sutras became the most translated text of the medieval era, translated into about forty Indian languages and two non-Indian languages: Old Javanese and Arabic. The text fell into relative obscurity for nearly 700 years but made a comeback in the late 19th century when Swami Vivekananda, the Theosophical Society, Paramahamsa Yogananda and others brought the science of yoga over to the West.

Of course, there is not just one source of information for yoga and where it originated from since it is part of an ocean of information which emanated from the heart of ancient Indian culture and philosophy. The ingenuity of Patanjali's Yoga Sutras lies in how he compiled all of the important aspects of Yoga practice into a succinct sutra or treatise. Patanjali refers to the 5 main texts from which he studied and learnt the principles of yoga – *The Bhagavad Gita, The Vedas, The Upanishads,* Svatmarama's *Hatha Yoga Pradipika* and the *Yoga Korunta* (a Nepalese scripture), not claiming the systems to be his own but bringing them all together. You could call him the founder of mixed yoga arts.

When compiling this information into his own system, he categorised those 196 sutras or aphorisms into 4 main chapters, which became the magnificent treatise he called the **Yoga Sutras**;

- **Samadhi Pada** - 51 sutras, on the art of becoming and staying blissful
- **Sadhana Pada** - 55 sutras, on the sciences of Kriya and Ashtanga Yoga
- **Vibhuti Pada** - 56 sutras, on the gaining of Siddhis (supernatural powers)
- **Kaivalya Pada** - 34 sutras, on emancipation or liberation

The first Yoga recommended by Patanjali is *Kriya* Yoga, more notably propagated by the late Paramahansa Yogananda, a man with a brilliant mind who shook the world with his revelations into the meaning and practice of breath control.

Kriya yoga is comprised of the following:

***Tapas** – austerity and persisting effort*
Yoga is a spiritual journey that cleanses the mind and body of *samskara*, or destructive habits and patterns. They are the embodiments of our thoughts and personality manifested, and we can become very identified with them, making them extraordinarily difficult to change. Tapas describes the persisting effort to burn away these "impurities" which block us from seeing our own true nature, it is the "heat" with which we conduct our rituals and disciplines. You could call it a consistent striving. It is not to say we are impure in the eyes of God or compared to anyone else, but that we are impure in our own sense and reasoning, when we are stuck in the loops of samskara and the grand illusion maya.

***Svādhyaya** – study of scriptures and self*
Since Yoga is also of the mind and not just of the body, we are encouraged to learn about our true nature through self-study, logic, reasoning and intelligence as well as practicing the disciplines of physical yoga and meditation.

***Iśvara praṇidhana** – devotion to God or pure consciousness*
I feel that this is self-explanatory, each person having their own take on what they consider this to be. For the faithful it's between you and your God, for the atheist, it's between the world and yourself. As they say in Thailand, "Same same, but different."

These 3 principles are also included under *niyama* (virtues) in the second Yoga recommended by Patanjali called *Ashtanga* Yoga, "the Eight-

Limbed science". Ashtanga was propagated heavily by Patanjali and also by a later Saint and Yogi by the name of Krishnamacharya, who made considerable efforts under the request of the King of Mysore at that time to establish a school for Yogic education in south India. The last disciple of this lineage is BNS Iyengar, who at the time of writing this book is still actively teaching in Mysore today.

The **Eight Limbs of Ashtanga yoga** are known as:

- *Yama* (abstinences)

- *Niyama* (observances)

- *Asana* (yoga postures)

- *Pranayama* (breath control)

- *Pratyahara* (withdrawal of the senses)

- *Dharana* (concentration)

- *Dhyana* (meditation)

- *Samadhi* (absorption in bliss-state)

These limbs were written in order, so that one can progress through them as a course of rites to ultimate self-awareness.

Niyama/Yama
The niyama and yama are a moral code, a set of things we are advised to do and not to do respectively – in this way the yamas are similar to the 7 deadly sins of Christianity, and the niyamas are like the virtues of man expounded upon by Christ. For this reason I shall not preach about them except to explain how they can be useful to one's own personal development, as opposed to judging or branding people.

Niyama (Virtues/Observations)

- *Saucha* (cleanliness) – *Shat Kriya* is the manual process by which this is done, including for example *Nadi Shodhana* (*nadi* cleansing), *Neti* (airway cleansing) and *Nauli/Dhouti* (abdominal wall/intestinal cleansing).

- *Santosha* (contentment)

- *Tapas* (discipline, austerity or 'burning enthusiasm)

- *Svadhyaya* (study of the self and of the texts)

- *Isvara Pranidhana* (surrender to a higher being, or contemplation of a higher power)

Yama (Restraints/Abstinences)

- *Ahimsa* (non-harming or non-violence in thought, word and deed)

- *Satya* (non-lying, truthfulness)

- *Asteya* (non-stealing)

- *Brahmacharya* (celibacy or 'correct use of energy')

- *Aparigraha* (non-greed or non-hoarding)

Asana *(Postures)*

Now we come to what is more commonly known not just in the West but across the world now, as Yoga. *Asana* are postures that one can hold for a period of time. Patanjali does not list any specific asana, except loosely suggesting they are,

> "Postures one can hold with comfort and motionlessness.
> "Asanas are perfected over time by relaxation of effort with meditation on the infinite." – **Verse 2.47, Yoga Sutras**

This combination of practice stops the quivering of body, allowing us to find the concept of stillness and the space created by it through our practice. What we have now done with Yoga in the West is to make it all about an impossible series of bone-bending postures in the pursuit of ability and performance. It is stated in the Yoga Sutras that intense practising of Asana can lead to the development of Siddhis (supernatural powers), however they also warn in Verse 3.37 that these powers can become an obstacle to the yogi who seeks liberation if he obsesses with them.

In Patanjali's commentary attached to the Yoga Sutras called **Bhasya**, he suggests twelve seated meditation postures:

- *Padmasana* (lotus)

- *Virasana* (hero)

- *Bhadrasana* (glorious)

- *Svastikasana* (lucky mark)

- *Dandasana* (staff)

- *Sopasrayasana* (supported)

- *Paryankasana* (bedstead)

- *Krauncha-nishadasana* (seated heron)

- *Hastanishadasana* (seated elephant)

- *Ushtranishadasana* (seated camel)

- *Samasansthanasana* (evenly balanced)

- *Sthirasukhasana* (any motionless posture that is in accordance with one's pleasure)

The last asana mentioned, Sthira-sukh-asana, literally translates as "steady-easy-posture". It's of particular interest to me since it does away with the myth that we must be seated to meditate, it allows us the power to choose our own position be that sitting, standing or laying down. This reference alone expanded my understanding of the many ways that we meditate in the modern era without even knowing that we are doing it. It is not happening when we "space out" – this is more akin to simply being unconscious of your surroundings while awake, but not necessarily conscious and aware while awake, otherwise known as being in a meditative state. Hence why when people catch you spacing out you aren't usually aware that you are doing it until snapped out of it. When we consciously become motionless and still within ourselves the material world temporarily dissolves away from our awareness by our own will, even though we are sitting right in it. Spacing out therefore is a sign of the mind trying to forcibly leave the senses – it is the soul telling us that we need time away from the constantly incoming feedback of the body and mind.

Prāṇāyāma *(Breath control)*
The word Pranayama is formed from two Sanskrit words *prāṇa* (प्राण, breath) and *āyāma* (आयाम, restraining, extending, stretching). In verses 2.49 through 2.51 the Yoga Sutras state that once a desired posture has been achieved, the next limb of yoga *prāṇāyāma* should be employed, which is the practice of consciously regulating the inhalation and exhalation of the breath. As with the previously mentioned asana, pranayama is recommended as a series of advancing practices which are best taught by a professional to avoid undesirable effects, since if the extreme breathing techniques are performed by an unprepared practitioner they can cause light headedness and dizziness or even loss of consciousness. You wouldn't put a child in the water and tell them to hold their breath – their lungs and heart are too weak to withstand the pressure of that activity, they aren't prepared for it yet. In the odd case that they have talent or a genetic advantage then maybe, but generally no. So too you don't put an adult who has immature breath control into advanced breathing programmes. The student must dedicate himself to the process gradually but thoroughly.

There are **14 yogic breaths** referred to across the Yoga Sutras and other texts. They are;

- *Natural breathing*
- *Basic Abdominal breathing*
- *Thoracic breathing*
- *Clavicular breathing*
- *Yogic breathing* (Kundalini)
- *Deep breathing with ratios* (Kriya Kundalini)
- *Interrupted breathing* (Viloma)
- *Alternate Nostril breathing* (AnulomVilom)
- *Heating breath* (Kapalbhati)
- *Cooling breath* (Sitkari)
- *Victorious breath* (Ujjayi)
- *Humming Bee breath* (Bhramari)
- *Bellow's breath* (Bhastrika)
- *Solar breath* (Surya Bhedan)

With so many techniques available and such detailed progression routes, what is the real significance of a breathing practice? Yogananda's Guru, Swami Sri Yushtekwar explained to his students; "The ancient Yogi's discovered that the secret of cosmic consciousness is intimately linked with breath mastery, this is India's unique and deathless contribution to the world's treasury of knowledge."

I know it might seem a cheat to let someone else explain it for me, but I could not do it more justice than the following golden excerpts from Paramahamsa Yogananda's 150,000 word book published 1946, "Autobiography of a Yogi";

> "Kriya Yoga is an ancient science. It is a psychophysiological method by which human blood is decarbonated and recharged with oxygen...
>
> ...Illustrations can be given to demonstrate the mathematical relationship between man's respiratory rate and the variations in his state of consciousness (e.g. wholly engrossed in study, in emotional states, during physical feats, etc.)...
>
> ...through mastery of the breath, the Yogi arrests decay in the body by quietening the actions of the lungs and heart, thereby securing an additional supply of prana (life force). He also arrests mutations of growth by controlling apana (the eliminating current/dissolving force), this neutralising decay and ageing...
>
> ...the restless monkey breathes at a rate of 32 times a minute, man at an average of 18. The giant tortoise, who can attain the age of 300 years, breathes only 4 times a minute...
>
> ...the body of a man is like a 50 watt lamp which cannot accommodate the billion watts of power roused by an excessive practice of Kriya. Through gradual and regular increase of the simple and foolproof methods of Kriya, man's body becomes astrally transformed day to day, and is finally fit to express the infinite potentials of cosmic energy which constitute the first materialistic expression of spirit."

Pratyahara *(Withdrawal of the senses)*
Pratyābāra is a combination of two Sanskrit words *prati-* परति, ("against" or "contra") and *ābāra* आहार, ("food, diet or intake")

Pratyahara is the self-imposed limitation and withdrawal from the never ending stimuli of the 5 senses. It is a process of letting go of our identifications with what we see, what we hear, what we eat and so on. It is of course impossible to do this constantly because otherwise your physical body would die, but doing so as a regular process or activity for short periods of time is similar to what happens when we go to sleep – we are temporarily relieved of the mind's processes in dealing with incoming information, allowing us to use that cognitive power for healing in the cosmic currents and deeper realisations of meditation. So you could call pratyahara the training by which one removes themselves from the ever-transient outer experience in order to move closer to that of the full meditative inner-experience known as Samadhi (bliss-state).

Dharana *(Concentration)*
Dharana धारणा means concentration, introspective focus and one-pointedness of mind. The root of word is *dhr* धृ, which has a meaning of "to hold, maintain, keep".

Dharana is the sixth limb of Ashtanga yoga and essentially means to be able to fixate one's mind onto a task. It is also to be able to hold space – that is, to be able to create room for a particular line of thought/emotion, or withdrawal of thought/emotion.

Mantra are commonly used as a tool for aiding concentration on the meditative experience, such as the omniscient sound of AUM ॐ. Mantra are set words or groups of words which are chanted to a certain rhythm and tune, alongside deep breathing and long extended sounds in order to maximise the healing and transformative properties of the vibrations created. These vibrations permeate every cell in the body and make shifts in the natural biological, chemical, physical and electromagnetic structures of the cells. This is mainly due to the effects that vibration has on water – the water content of the cells is what enables them to have malleability and hold memory, they can be influenced and manipulated by use of vibration. Light frequencies can also have the same effects although by working on a more subtle level, since we cannot "feel" light but we can feel sound because the vibration is at a frequency we can detect physically. Amplified light frequencies for example are usually felt as certain types of heat. Amplified sound is usually felt more as what we know of commonly to be vibration.

A form of meditation typically used to help concentration through light frequency is *Trataka* (fire staring), which exercises the muscles of the eyes and helps us to create and maintain *dhristi*, or focused gaze. The light gives us a focal point and anchor for space and time, so we can bring ourselves back to it when the mind or body begins to distract us during the meditation.

Dhyana *(Meditation)*

Dhyana ध्यान literally means "contemplation, reflection on the profound and abstract"

Dharana, or concentration, is not meditativeness. It is the means by which we can come to the process of meditation. Concentration is being fully engrossed in and focused on your task. Meditation has no focus or task, but none the less is still engrossed in the flow. It is allowing oneself to be at one with oneself, to be taskless so that the process simply runs by itself.

In his own commentary of the *Yoga Sutras*, Indian saint and philosopher Adi Shankara gives the example that a Yogi in a state of Dharana (concentration) on the morning sun is aware of its features and marvels at all of this. The Yogi in Dhyana (meditation) however, "contemplates on the sun's orbit alone for example, without being interrupted by its colour, brilliance or other related ideas", according to Trevor Leggett. The Yogi is able to continue his line of inquiry without any other permutation of thought interrupting his thinking process, that process being truth seeking.

Samadhi *(Absorption)*

The final 8th limb of Yoga is *Samadhi* समाधि literally meaning "to put together, join, combine with, union, harmonious whole, trance". We see the word union used here, which is what I referred to as being closest in interpretation to the word Yoga.

Now how does one explain what being in Samadhi actually is? From a Yogic perspective, I would say it can be described as the holding of a non-judgemental space which is impervious and impenetrable to the external world, whereby we can find liberation in the absolute stillness, and contemplate on that bliss of just being, which is above all of this doing.

Samadhi is a state of being neither separable nor inseparable to bliss. It is simply being in it. Now we can only do this when we fully let go of everything, and I mean everything. We have to be able to shake off absolutely every last piece of tension, acting, mediating and emotion. This is an extremely hard thing to do at the click of a finger, and that is exactly why the process of Yoga was invented. To guide us through a set of rites and rituals which can ultimately, through process alone, bring us to that space where we can experience Samadhi, union with the ultimate bliss state, where there is no beginning or end, no cycles of birth and death (*karma*), just oneness, *moksha*, liberation.

Thus, Yoga is not the practice of just one aspect, but the entire process, from beginning to end. I could summarise the entire Yogic process this way;

Firstly, we start with those observances and abstinences that make us more aware of how well we are looking after and treating ourselves and others. We then move onto *asana*, which is defined not as just postures, but those rituals described for function, health, worship and meditation, such as the famous *Surya Namaskar* (Sun Salutation) or Neti Kriya (cleansing techniques). The 11 recommend postures we can meditate in easily included a twelfth which gave us the freedom to choose any other posture which is conducive to our meditation. All else is impressive but not foundational.

Once we find our stillness in the positions, we become aware of the breath. The breath carries the life current. We begin to learn the control of this breath and thus the flow of prana. When we have established control of the breath, the lungs and heart get stronger thus reducing the accumulation of venous blood. This allows the body to sit longer without discomfort, keeps blood flowing and prepares the body to begin learning the art of meditation.

The first step in learning meditation is to practice withdrawing ourselves from the outward world by cutting off the 5 senses and incoming stimuli. Then in that space we have created, where the mind's chatter has dissipated, we learn concentration which is a focused group of thoughts. Once we are able to control what our mind is concentrating on, we can direct that concentration from the thoughts themselves to the observer of the thoughts, the part of us which is monitoring ourselves, checking in on our actions and thoughts. The role of being "the Observer", not the thinker or doer, is the same as being in the process of meditation. When this process has finally been learnt, through the rigorous, dedicated and devoted practice and heart of the Yogi, a miracle occurs – by using meditation as his tool, he can enter the state of Samadhi at will. In this state, he is beyond this world, in a state of bliss beyond life's troubles and so, beyond death. This is the Yoga of India.

This Yoga, alongside countless other disciplines including Ayurvedic physical therapy, medicine and surgery, philosophy, science, politics, economics, sociology, architecture, astronomy, performing arts, literature and martial arts make India one of, if not the richest ancient cultures of the world. If you follow martial arts, you will see that Thai boxing (Muay Thai), the Fighting Art of 8 Limbs, was formed from a more ancient art called Muay Boran. In this old style, there is a prayer ritual performed inside the ring to banish evil spirits and to pay respect to one's teacher (Kru in Thai, Guru in Sanskrit), as well as offering prayer to Buddha, Hanuman and Lord Rama (Vishnu's 7th avatar). That particular set of movements is called Wai Kru Ram Muay and is still in use today, you will see most if not all the boxers of Thai origin doing it before a bout.

The interesting connection is not just the similarity in name 8 limbs of Yoga with 8 limbs of Muay, but also the use of the word Ram in the name of the ritual. Lord Ram or Rama was not just thought to be an avatar of Vishnu but a very real man who was an Indian king, revered so much for his righteous nature and actions that he was considered an avatar of God. His most loyal devotee, Hanuman, who I have mentioned many times already, is revered and noted by the Thai's as the inspiration for Muay Boran and Ram Muay, with their movements and style imitating that of the half-human half-monkey avatar.

Hence, the connections of the Vedas and the Yogic texts of India with other world cultures continue to be affirmed and understood in new ways, their context and value increasing more and more as we enter a new dawn of self-awareness and technology.

CHAPTER 4
Sport Science, Concepts and Programming

Conversely to the Yogic and Vedic sciences, if we were to look at the practice of scientific method that developed in Western Europe we can also delve into the academic hypotheses (claims), methods (rituals) and conclusions (realisations) which have helped to shape our modern understanding of the world. In this chapter I draw particular focus to the sciences regarding the human body, such as biology, biochemistry, kinesiology, physiotherapy, osteopathy, etc. My reason for this is because in the context of human development, we should apportion more weight and significance to those sciences which have conclusions we can integrate into our daily lives regardless of our profession. That is, to make science useful for the average person. The selection of information in this chapter is dedicated to compiling some of that together into a meaningful message about what we as humans can do to maintain our health and wellbeing.

So it would be fitting to start with introduction to what sport science is and how it was developed in the West, followed by some of the latest concepts and breakthroughs for working past previous limitations and moving towards high performance.

It would make sense to first start with what sport science is and where the practice originates from. Sport science is defined as a discipline which studies how the healthy human body functions during movement and effort, as well as how sport and physical activity promote health and performance overall. Bangor University describes it as an academic subject that includes the scientific study of physiology, psychology, motor control and biomechanics. Most run-of-the-mill fitness advice such as "it's bad for your knees to squat past 90 degrees" or "you shouldn't eat carbs" is built from outdated understandings and hearsay which sport science has debunked, rightly so. Sport science has offered us a method for applying the intellect to the performance of the human body – we do in fact, owe a great debt to it in consideration of the enlightenment received regarding the physical potentials of the human being.

So it can be said that the study of sport science is generally lead by therapists and doctors who have taken a specific interest in the human application of the sciences they work with, although notable coaches and athletes have of course been heavily involved in the interpretations and assumptions made. This uniting of real life doers with theoretical thinkers has given us the wonderful insight and knowledge we now know as sport science.

Programming and Performance
Most of what we have covered in this book so far has been about learning processes which help us to hold onto that which keeps us happy, healthy and human. But what about the striving we have as a human race to progress? To see the unbound limitations of man explored in depth as we marvel at the feats of talented athletes, musicians, dancers and actors? What limits us in being able to use our bodies the way we want to? When it comes to physical performance for sporting and competitive purposes, we have a whole different ball game to play.

It's not always just lack of ability – often times it's actually dysfunction, meaning that the body is not operating efficiently to its designed biomechanics, or that it is not sufficiently conditioned to be carrying out the activities that it is doing. How is dysfunction caused? Well dysfunction is also known as subconsciously and physically stored trauma, inherited from previous injury or upset to the person on any of the physical, mental and emotional planes. For instance, a person who has been emotionally scorned protects their heart with cross-armed postures as a psychophysiological defence mechanism. A child who accidentally broke a bone did not rehabilitate it and learnt to subconsciously protect that area by compensating the effort to other parts of the body, carrying that imbalance through to adulthood. A person who was violently abused by bullies can become defensive and insecure in the mind and body if that emotion is not dealt with.

When we consider how we might understand and heal our traumas and dysfunctions, the closest discipline that offers a holistic perspective on the performance of the human body is osteopathy. Osteopathy was coined as a practice in the late 18th century by Physician and Surgeon Dr. Andrew Taylor Still, the son of a Methodist preacher. Still stated that in order to achieve the highest possible form of health, all parts of the body should work together harmoniously. Osteopathy brings into practice a holistic view of the musculoskeletal system alongside the nervous system, endocrine (hormonal) systems and more in order to diagnose and treat a patient with manual therapy techniques.

Physiotherapy on the other hand, limited to the skeletomuscular system, has its earliest documented origins in 1813. Physical manipulation of the musculoskeletal system and exercise was advocated by the father of Swedish gymnastics, Per Henrik Ling, who also founded the Royal Central Institute of Gymnastics. The first official physiotherapy research was published in the United States in 1921 in The PT Review, and in the same year Mary McMillan organized the Physical Therapy Association (now called the American Physical Therapy Association (APTA) which regulates the discipline.

A very relevant concept across these disciplines is *neuroplasticity*, which states that nerve growth or loss (pruning) is a result of usage or non-usage, respectively. The significance of this concept is in our ability to directly manipulate and train the nervous system to learn wanted habits and lose unwanted ones. We can do this today more accurately because of sport science, using a range of hacks, systems and therapies to subtly or aggressively adjust dysfunctional patterns across all states of human health (mind, body, emotional and spiritual). There are of course other fields of study or disciplines such as acupuncture, reflexology, etc. which are not accepted by science or called "alternative therapy" as if in some way to reduce them from being as valid as other forms of logic-based therapy. But the fact is they are only considered less scientific because they work on the bio-electromagnetic system of the body which is not accepted in medical science.

From this we can reason that most if not all physical dysfunction originates from trauma and the subsequent improper healing of said trauma. As I mentioned before there are many forms of therapy that help us to rehabilitate, both ancient and new, but what about the tools for improving performance in a world of competitive sport and combat? Let's take the shining example of competition that is the combatant, or the martial artist – the martial artist is not great because of his volume of techniques, even though that does give him variety in options. A martial artist is great because he can execute the techniques he has, no matter how few, with outstanding accuracy, timing and to devastating effect, or controlled effect. It's not to go as far as to say handicaps such as tying one arm can be accounted for, but if a person has all their limbs available for defence and can use only one attack perfectly, they have a chance to prevail so long as they can keep defending well. They just need the one chance for their attack to land, and if the attack has been honed with expert use, it can prevail.

> *"I don't fear the man who has practiced a thousand kicks, I fear the man who has practiced one kick a thousand times."* **– Bruce Lee**

After much practice of a set pattern or thought (today's science estimates around 10,000 repetitions), the body begins to perform the task without the need to bother the brain too much. This type of memory is stored in the body as a loop or reflexive pattern. Repeating something is therefore a way of educating the cells, tissues and nervous system of the body to store memory, which yields more efficient programmed action to stimuli rather than sporadic reaction. So in a functional and therapeutic way, repetition of physical movement can be seen as a method for manipulating and evolving cell, tissue, nerve and mind based memory. It is a powerful tool for grooving and re-grooving patterns, or set reactions. To be able to adapt physically and mentally, many times within a lifetime.

Any movement of the body is a combination of specific nervous system and muscle fibre recruitment in specific muscles with specific intensities, moving through specific angles and planes of space at a specific rate of time. What this means is that every time you move, it's impossible to replicate that movement exactly again. Each time you're creating a unique movement that has never been done like that before – if we analysed it with a super-computer there would always be some element of change somewhere in the body. That's why in any group of people doing the same movements, each person will perform it in their own distinctive way. It will always be distinct from any other if you look hard enough - it's even distinct from anything they did before themselves. So the purpose of any practice is therefore to either maximise or limit how much variance we produce, decided mainly by the function that the movement is being performed for.

When we look at the effects of using enhanced technique in performance, it offers a far greater set of benefits than seeking raw power. Raw power could be described as physical strength. Technique however not only minimises any strength discrepancy and energy wastage, it can also take advantage of an opponent's disadvantages. Moreover, there is spiritual power, emotional intensity and the passion behind a person's movement. A person's reasons are of course hugely important, like the Indian saint Gandhi said *"Strength does not come from physical capacity. It comes from indomitable will power in the heart"*.

I want to make clear that I am saying both willpower and technique are needed, in equal measure. Or as other big inspirations of mine have said;

"You have inspiration, but then you have to have technique, to incarnate, to express your inspiration. That is to say, to bring a piece of Heaven down to Earth, and to express Heaven in terms of Earth. Of course they are really one behind the scenes, but there is no way of pointing it out unless you do something skillful."
– Alan Watts

"Strength does not come from winning. Your struggles develop your strength. When you go through hardships and decide not to surrender, that is strength."
– Arnold Schwarzenegger

Concerning belt ranks for martial arts:

"It doesn't matter what you have around your waist, what counts is what is in your hands and your heart." **– Garry Lever, Gu-Do; A Hunger for the Way**

So if the body is not physically prepared to manifest and execute the mind and soul's desires, we cannot perform. It's very similar to the analogy of Yogananda – the average person being like a lamp with a 50-watt voltage, needing to train the body if they want to be able to receive the billions of watts of cosmic energy available. So I hold that it is of utmost importance to make fit this vessel called the body for its intended use. That intended use is whatever you decide it is, because it's your life and your body.

"Human joints have to withstand considerable forces day to day from compression, shearing and tension. Movement and stress always result in mechanical deformation of tissues and structures in the body because tissues undergo an elastic deformation when they are stretched. This deformation allows the tissue to rebound to its original shape and length if it is stretched within normal limits. However, if the tissue is stressed beyond its physical limitations of the elastic phase, it will fail to return to its original structure and will be lengthened. We call this the plastic phase of deformation." **– Threlkeld 1992**

Threlkeld's paper introduces to us of another important concept in sport science, where the body is responding to stresses and forces placed upon it through practice, use and overuse. *Mechanotransduction*, a term pinned by the great scientists Khan and Scott in their journal paper "Mechanotherapy: how physical therapists' prescription of exercise promotes tissue repair" of 2009. This enlightening and insightful piece of research eloquently explains that mechanotransduction is the physiological process where cells sense and respond to mechanical loads. This paper reclaims the term "mechanotherapy" and presents the current scientific knowledge underpinning how load may be used therapeutically to stimulate tissue repair and remodelling in tendon, muscle, cartilage and bone.

Essentially what this paper surmises is that the body responds to forces and load constantly, not just when we consciously use it. Thus, mechanotransduction is actually a process, which is happening all the time just like breathing (the process of respiration) and digestion (process of metabolism). The body does this via 3 stages, outlined further in the paper;

1. Mechanocoupling – described in Khan and Scotts paper as "the direct or indirect physical perturbation of the cell, which is transformed into a variety of chemical signals both within and among cells." Meaning that when a physical force or load is placed upon the body, a chemical reaction happens in the local cells.

2. **Cell to cell communication** – the stage where cells communicate details and information about the load to the nervous system and the other physical cells across the body.

3. **Effector cell response** – detailing the body's cellular level response to the force or load, which may take the form of scarring, tissue building or regeneration, motor path development, etc.

Why this is so significant for sport science today is that mechanotransduction details at the most micro-level we have investigated to date, what happens in the body when you put the pressure of training and exercise on it.

"Mechanotherapy was first defined in 1890 as "the employment of mechanical means for the cure of disease" (Oxford English Dictionary). We would update this to "the employment of mechanotransduction for the stimulation of tissue repair and remodelling." This distinction highlights the cellular basis of exercise prescription for tissue healing and also recognises that injured and healthy tissues may respond differently to mechanical load." – **Khan & Scott, 2009**

Using this information and further details we can arrive at a whole host of techniques and processes by which the human body's abilities can be improved for the highest level of performance. During the 1950's, Dr. Fred L. Mitchell Sr coined the concept of "Muscle Energy Technique", a set of manual therapy methods whereby a therapist would ask the patient to use force into and away from the direction of the joint manipulation. These techniques have lead to great innovations in the development of rehabilitation and performance development. More recently, Dr. Andreo Spina took this concept amongst others further by creating the Functional Range Systems, whereby a set of bases, positions and techniques were taken from various yoga, martial arts and sport disciplines in order to make therapeutic use of them in accordance with the latest sport science principles.

So when it comes to performance there are many things we can take into account, such as speed, power, strength, stability/balance, adaptiveness, mobility, flexibility, rhythm, etc. Sport science has made absolute leaps and bounds in the last 20 years in terms of how we can hack and train the body to yield these benefits and abilities, but time and time again when we look at this data, we can see that one of the most key components in high performance is having the requisite mobility and control for the positions which are part of whatever movement we are doing.

Range of active motion or "mobility" is not directional, it is either curved, circular or ovular in fashion, even at hinge joints (elbows and knees). Nothing moves in perfectly straight lines, there is always some level of rotation or bending at the joints and an arc of movement, which helps us explore the subtle curved deviances of a basic line or square movement.

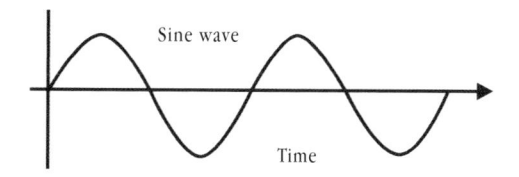

Sine wave

Time

There are lines, and then there are sine waves, which deviate to each side of the line in a wave pattern. You could call the sine wave, the breathing of the line. Then when you connect lines together at different angles you have different shapes – and then there is the breathing of the lines within those shapes. You could try to imagine your lungs represented by cubes, inflating with air and then deflating. The lines of the cubes will bend inwards or outwards, adapting to the forces and fixed tension at the corners to hold shape.

What I'm saying here is that once we have enough ability to make position in correct form (the stable line), if we are to use it in any functional movements we have to first learn how to use the breathing in and breathing out of that line, the sine wave, which we achieve through training for range of motion, articulated control and fluidity of control. This is called mobility and range of motion training.

Mobility and end-range conditioning is the athletic enhancement and conditioning of the joints to perform at longer ranges and extreme angles, which benefits the athlete by creating more efficiency in their movements and gives them more options for how to move. Say you're skiing and you hit an unexpected bump, or playing basketball and someone tries to cross you fast. Your ability to react and have options for your reaction are entirely dependent on the range of mobility and control you have of your spine, limbs and joints. All motion starts with the core firing to create structural tension, whilst the spine and limbs are for directing force into desired planes of movement.

Finally, I present as summary a scale on which we all sit – a scale with two polarities, trauma and high performance. Since these two sit on opposite ends, we can organise all of the medical and physical therapists towards the trauma side of the line, surgery being at the extreme end and therapy/rehabilitation towards the middle. The yoga teachers, biomechanical and corrective exercise coaches would be more in the middle, with high performance or strength/sports coaches at the other end. Granted many individuals have learnt more than one discipline so they would cover a range of skills on the line rather than just one role, which is exactly why I believe that a more holistic knowledge of the body is required for anyone in these roles.

We have coaches doing more damage than help injuring their clients with things they are not ready for, simply because of a lack of the required knowledge around maintenance, care and healing of muscles, joints and the nervous system. Then we have therapists who are excellent at diagnosing dysfunction but have relatively little idea about how athletes actually use their bodies in sport, since the therapist often does not have a physical practice of their own. Everybody that works with individual people on their physical health and ability needs to always be upskilling, improving their understanding of the body in all aspects even if they don't work in those areas. This will ensure that we are to useful and helpful not only to our clients and patients, but to ourselves also. This is not just limited to the realm of medical and sport science – it is a fundamental observance that needs to change across the world.

Biohacking
My good friend Tim Gray introduced me to a concept called Biohacking shortly before asking me to present at the World Health Optimisation Summit 2019, which he founded and runs each year in London. Being one of the world's leading experts on the matter, he introduced me to the concepts of others leading the way in the field including Dave Asprey. Biohacking can be summarised as the use of technology or natural life hacks to heal, repair and maintain optimal performance of the human being. It is a thought-leading industry, well researched and forward looking in terms of pushing for more research and studies into the use of technology for human health. It does however open up a myriad of questions regarding its practitioners who are sometimes considered to

be chasing highs, obsessive with tracking their biostatistics or being over-dependant on external technology for their wellbeing.

To give an overview of what biohacking includes I have broken it down into 3 main categories or areas of study:

1. **Psychophysiological tools**
   The means by which a person uses psychological and physiological methods to enhance their level of perception and consciousness, through both physical and mentally directed activities.

2. **Bio-chemical tools**
   The means by which a person ingests, uses or applies organic and inorganic chemicals for the purpose of improving health and performance.

3. **Bio-electromagnetic tools**
   The means by which a person uses vibrations, frequencies and energy to heal, repair and maintain the electromagnetic balance inside and outside the body.

There are several practices that are now well understood and scientifically verified, for example blue-light blocking sunglasses which block the high frequency blue light our electric cities are flooded with. Blocking this particular frequency of light from our eyes at certain times helps our body tune into its circadian rhythms better as it responds to natural light, for instance as the sun goes down we are designed to also begin the night's rest after a hard day of work. The concept of grounding, standing barefoot outside so as to swap positive electrons from your body with the Earth which is a huge reserve and bank of negative electrons. Positive electrons in our body are the result of the numerous radiowaves, cellphone signals and other forms of EMF radiation that our bodies are exposed to on a daily basis. Regular exposure to positive electrons causes oxidisation of the cells, which in turn can lead to the production of free radicals (unstable atoms). These atoms cause damage and kill our cells, which is why the government health information always advises inclusion of "anti-oxidants" in the diet. Antioxidants stop mutations of growth by helping to restore the electromagnetic balance in our cells and avoid the production of free radicals in the body.

Biohackers often pay particular attention to the brain and how we can "hack it" to produce a different experience - alertness, concentration, better sleep, etc. A study by Neuroscientist Richard Davidson investigated the brains of olympic level meditators (62000+ hours of meditation) who lived in Nepal/India and were put through state of the art tests at his lab in the University of Wisconsin, USA. Normally, humans experience something called a gamma wave, which flows over the brain for a brief second when you are experiencing something intensely, for instance biting into an apple or even imagining doing that. The taste, sound, smell and vision all combines to create a very short period of experiental intensity, lasting only a second or so in normal brain activity.

Remarkably, the brain waves of the meditation experts showed active gamma waves flowing across the brain all the time. It's simply their every day state of mind. What's more, when asked to do a meditation on compassion their gamma levels jumped 700-800%! Science has never seen anything like it before and does not understand what it means experientally, since they have no experienced it themselves. This points to the fact that there is a state of being which exists that is experienced totally differently to what we consider the norm.

Technologically we have even come as far as to have infra-red saunas where the heat penetrates straight into the cells instead of going through all the layers of body tissue as per with traditional heat based sauna. There are even mental performance supplements, herbal medicines which help counteract pain and dysfunction - as my friend Dr. Enayat showed me at one of his international high-performance clinics LMS Wellness in London, herbal tonics which combine ingredients such as Gopi Kola, Kapikachu and Rhodiola create infusions that can be used for different requirements such as alertness and restfulness, or even to mimic the effects of ecstasy in the body with natural serotonin enhancers.

Within these areas we have now reached developments in science which allow us to use far greater technology than we have ever had available. Most people in the world have access to a mobile phone now, and are connected to the internet which is an almost infinite source of information since it is in a live and constant state of update. If more spend allocation went towards the funding of research into how we can use technology to improve not just the general health level (organically) but also the accessibility to that technology, then we will be making great strides as humanity.

We know that our bodies can change and adapt to the environment. We can see that our bodies are undergoing a constant evolutionary process when we look at the proteins that are responsible for the growth, repair and development of the body. These functions are all coded by spliced RNA strands, which are coded by your DNA. Biologists have recently discovered that there are some RNA strands which are not used to code proteins, but to regulate the protein coding of other RNA strands. That activity is responsive to changes in your environmental and physical needs, so essentially this means you could change your own genetic makeup within a life cycle if you change your environment and the physical demands on your body.

There have also been accounts of human DNA "evolving", some people have now been born with 3 or 4 strands of DNA (!) compared to the regular 2 strand DNA most of us have. Although the function of those extra strands is not yet understood since it's a new phenomenon, we can assume that it is possible for new genes to be coded using these newly "awakened" strands. There are even people who say we can have up to 12 strands of DNA, as our bodies evolve further with the natural awakening of the Earth and our solar system.

"I used to think the top environmental problems were biodiversity loss, ecosystem collapse and climate change. I thought that with 30 years of good science we could address those problems, but I was wrong. The top environmental problems are selfishness, greed and apathy… …and to deal with those we need a spiritual and cultural transformation. We scientists don't know how to do that."
– Gus Speth, Environmental Scientist and Lawyer

CHAPTER 5

New Age Yoga: 7 Paths of Awakening

Yoga is called a *vijñana*, a science. Science is also aptly named thus, because it is ever evolving to best match the current requirement. This is why there are so many different yoga styles and variances in how it is taught. Both the Western and Yogic sciences are in constant evolution. They are not to be seen as unalterable commandments written in stone, but rather a set of previously established parameters for our own self-development and cosmological understanding of the modern world.

Those who are well versed in their particular styles of yoga will actually make some improvisations, which is allowed so long as it is within the fundamental framework which that style was originally structured around. When I say a Yoga scientist, I mean someone who has intensively studied the discipline and practiced/taught for many years. It would be foolish to begin adapting something if you had only just learnt the basics of the discipline. Notable Yogis who fit under this definition and made significant contributions to the evolution of Yoga include Krishnamacharya, Patthabi Jois, Yogananda, BKS Iyengar and RamDev.

Just because something is old, it doesn't become authentic or acceptable. Similarly, just because something is new, it doesn't become dispensable or discardable. It is only based on the merit of that work that you have to consider it. If a particular adaptation is truly helpful for practitioners in finding their way, then it need not be criticised. But we must not be naive - not all adaptations are helpful and some might even be detrimental to the student, like modifications introduced by unqualified teachers, or opportunistic people with ulterior motives. "Extraordinary claims require extraordinary evidence" was a phrase made popular by the famous Astrophysicist Carl Sagan, who reworded Laplace's principle which says "the weight of evidence for an extraordinary claim must be proportioned to its strangeness" (Gillispie et al., 1999).

Nearly all debates in epistemology are in some way related to knowledge. Most generally, "knowledge" is a familiarity, awareness, or understanding of someone or something, which might include facts (propositional knowledge), skills (procedural knowledge), or objects (acquaintance knowledge). Philosophers tend to draw an important distinction between three different senses of "knowing" something: "knowing that" (knowing the truth of propositions), "knowing how" (understanding how to perform certain actions), and "knowing by acquaintance" (directly perceiving an object, being familiar with it, or otherwise coming into contact with it). So the importance of being experienced as well as holding knowledge is huge and explicitly required for teaching.

So within the basic taught framework of any particular yoga style or sport, we can make innumerable innovations once we have come to better understand the depths of that style, so long as we do not disturb the core of the practice and can prove the benefits. This is why the transitions between postures give us a large element of room for creativity, since they were not documented as strongly as the set positions of the actual asana themselves. In Karate, Jiu-Jitsu and many other Eastern martial arts, the coloured belt rankings are meant for learning the foundations of the art. All ranks up to black belt are considered the foundational learning experience, but extra layers of knowledge, experience and contribution to the art are recognised by "Dan", which are extra notches on the black belt increasing in rank with each additional Dan, until a final 9th Dan is attained to denote Grandmaster status.

We only have to look at the concept of mixed disciplines to see that people can contribute by bringing technique and knowledge from other areas, blending the best of the best and discarding the rest. Martial arts has one such mixing of practices. Mixed martial arts or MMA as it is now commonly known, is considered the ultimate fighting style based on the ability of the practitioner to utilise several disciplines, allowing him to create infinite variations in style and combination. This makes them a more dangerous and difficult opponent to read or defeat, compared to a master of a single discipline is who not multi-dimensional and can therefore be predicted to a degree. So too over the ages have other arts mixed concepts from other arts with their own, the combined result yielding such legends as the "father of mixed martial arts" Bruce Lee.

Patanjali in his Yoga Sutras recommended joining the practices of Ashtanga Yoga and Kriya Yoga together, uniting two important and valid processes in order to yield more effective results. He mentions that combined simultaneous practice of dhāraṇā (concentration), dhyana (meditation) and samādhi (bliss-state) is referred to as *samyama*, and is considered a tool of achieving siddhis (supernatural powers). Krishnamacharya studied Patanjali's Yoga Sutras and other texts deeply, embodying them and eventually adding the separate branch and discipline of Vedic science *jnana* (knowledge seeking) to the mix. The Samkhya branch of Vedic science suggests that jnana is a sufficient means to moksha (liberation) by itself. Samkyha is the philosophy of Yoga, which is rarely studied or taught in enough depth in today's Yoga teacher trainings. The meaning behind the movements and why they are performed to certain order and effect is highly important. Patanjali and Krishnamachrya therefore both suggest that systematic techniques/ practice (personal experimentation) combined with Samkhya's approach to knowledge is the path to moksha (liberation).

So the aim of this chapter and part of the book is to present my own adapted, contemporary and holistic model for developing self-awareness and performance in the human being. For this I draw on my personal experiences of over 28 years multidisciplinary training, 20+ years of scientific study and 10 years of coaching people across the world from general public to world champions and other coaches/therapists. I hope you will find it a refreshing and insightful look into both old and new methods of awakening your true potential.

New Age Yoga: 7 Paths of Awakening

PATH	TYPE	POLARITY	SCIENCE	YOGA	PRIMARY BRAIN REGIONS
Breath	Spirit	+/−	Breath work, Therapy	Pranayama, Kriya	All
Healing	Body	−	Rehabilitation, Therapy	Yin Restorative, Ayurveda	Hypothalamus
Movement	Body	+	Exercise, Sport	Hatha, Vinyasa	Frontal lobes, Cerebellum
Astral	Mind	−	Meditation, Absorption	Dhyana, Samadhi	Amygdala, Pineal gland
Scholar	Mind	+	Concentration, Study of self	Dharana, Svadhyaya	Frontal lobes, Cerebral cortex
Rhythm	Emotion	−	Sound, Vibration	Mantra, Nada	Temporal lobes, Cerebellum
Tantric	Emotion	+	Self-control, Connection	Kundalini, Tantra	Amygdala, Pineal gland

What occurred to me when I devised these 7 Paths of New Age Yoga is that there have been brilliant historical accounts of people devising and detailing methods which they claim has lead them to samadhi, higher levels of self-awareness and increased performance. All of these paths, tested through to realisation by the masters who declared them, are therefore valid routes if they have been proven over time through a variety of people. To have them collected under one total system gives more options to the practitioner, utilising the cross-disciplinary method to speed the practitioner towards his or her goal, rather than doggedly pursuing just one path or option in hopes of redemption. Surely, we all have our own personal gifts and passions too, we must research ways to find them. We can be shown the ways, but we must walk the paths we choose. As a famous Zen saying goes *"there are many paths to the top of the mountain, but the view up there is the same"*.

So why 7 Paths as opposed to any other number? Well I give a lot of weight to the belief that the universe is modelled in first principles, mathematics and geometry. Numerology is the study of numerical patterns as related to events and sequences in our reality. The number 7 appears in many places, but some notable ones are:

- Lucky number 7, or 777
- The number of days of Genesis (Old Testament)
- The number of vital organs in the body
- The number of different colours (light frequencies) that split from white light through a prism
- The number of different notes (sound frequencies) in a full octave (C, D, E, F, G, A, B)
- The number of main chakras in the Yogic electromagnetic chart of the energy body (the total number is 114)
- The number of different planets in the original solar system before the arrival of Uranus, Neptune and Pluto

…and so on.

The polarities I have indicated for each path refer to the activation (+) or release (−) of a particular dimension or aspect of life and human nature, i.e. the Mind, Body, Emotion or Spirit. Since breath control is both inhalation and exhalation, both activating and releasing the life force, it carries both polarities. Perhaps that's why breath control is considered the most effective and efficient path, the Raja (Royal) Yoga. The other Paths express a certain aspect of human nature but with polarity, for instance an athlete may be strong in the activation (+) of body, but perhaps not in the release (−) of mind, or release (−) of emotion. Therefore I found it is of utmost importance for balance that we should cultivate multitasking other disciplines that have been proven timeless processes, regardless of age or origin. We are dedicated as human beings to progress and the process, not to blindly follow traditions or pseudo-sciences with no proof of effectiveness.

In order to follow each of these paths in the most organic way, I also recommend a further 7 tenets to observed in a particular order, whilst moving forward on any of the 7 Paths mentioned. That templated order is;

1. Purging (removal of trauma and healing of wounds)
2. Resetting (neutralisation and readying of the self for transformation, creating intention)
3. Initiation (taking the pledge and the first step forward)
4. Developing (dedicating to the process, honing the skills)
5. Integrating (bringing skills together, mastering the techniques of the art)
6. Expressing (bringing unique contribution to the art, mastering self-expression through it)
7. Fusing (merging the skills and lessons into the rest of your life)

Finally, 42 recommended yoga postures are provided which are fundamental positions I have handpicked to support and accommodate a person's development along the Paths. Each Path has 2 Series (A and B), a total of 6 postures which increase in difficulty. These positions systemised together form what I call New Age Yoga. By assigning specific postures to each Path, I am making a statement that the practice of postures is associated with and geared towards improving function, rather than just achieving the posture for the sake of it. When a movement or position has no purpose behind it, that's when it appears to be pointless or melodramatic. By that I don't mean that it has no function at all. I mean that there is no heart in any action without conviction. The conviction behind your movement is what makes you perform it in such a way that it inspires both you and everyone else who witnesses it, it is what makes it effective in function rather than simply doing it for its own sake.

Before I expound on the 7 Paths it's also recommended that one finds a guru, coach, teacher or mentor for whichever Paths they are choosing, since each one requires guidance, complex understanding and knowledge of how to apply certain sciences such as anatomy, biomechanics, music scales, maths, etc. The role of the guru is to help us navigate that unfamiliar terrain since they have been there and understand the deeper aspects of following these route/s.

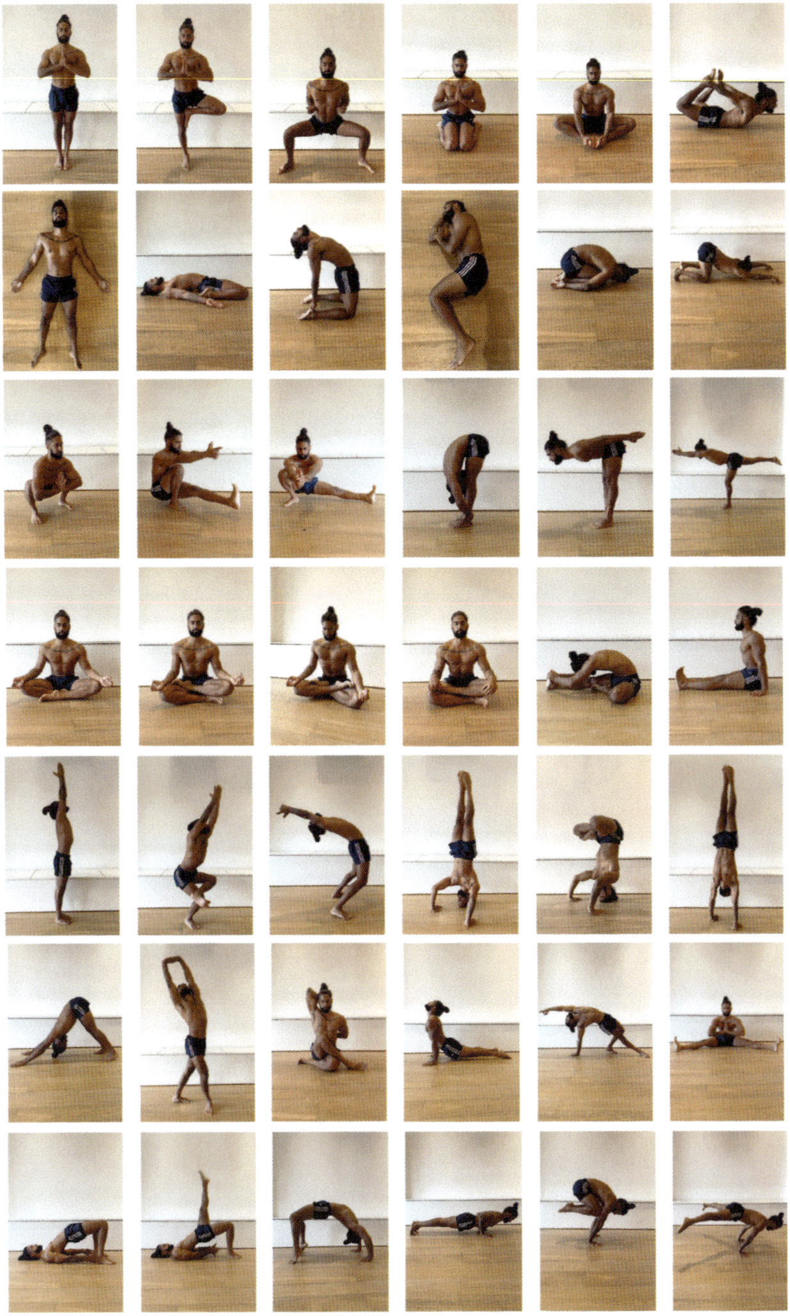

BREATH PATH

PATH	TYPE	POLARITY	SCIENCE	YOGA	PRIMARY BRAIN REGIONS
Breath	Spirit	+/−	Breath work Therapy	Pranayama, Kriya	All

SERIES A:

Pranamasana (Prayer)

Eka Pada Pranamasana (One-legged Prayer)

Utkata Konasana (God/Goddess)

SERIES B:

Virasana (Hero)

Baddha Konasana (Cobbler)

Dhanurasana (Bow)

SERIES A: Begins with the easy, resting position *Pranamasana*. Here we can begin to learn stillness and calmness while we focus on the breath in a standing position, with the hands in front of the heart in gratitude. *Eka Pada Pranamasana* adds the requirement for better balance during breathing practice and should be practiced on both sides. *Utkata Konasana* lowers the centre of gravity thus strengthening the legs, as well as increasing the demands on the heart.

SERIES B: Begins with *Virasana*, an easy seated posture for breathing. A cushion under the knees or between the feet and bottom increases comfort. Moving on to *Baddha Konasana*, we learn active posture for the spine whilst opening the hip girdle to maximise diaphragm expansion. A challenging final posture, *Dhanurasana* teaches us to breathe whilst actively tensing the posterior chain and opening the chest, but it also places the diaphragm under extreme restriction due to the floor pressing up against it – this trains the muscles of the ribs and core to strengthen whilst lengthening.

As I've mentioned, breath control is the Raja (Royal) Yoga. The beauty of this path and why it deserves to be first is that it is the most simple and accessible path that anyone can follow. It is an ingenious process by which someone can get to know oneself purely through process. It requires no specific talent or intelligence, simply the dedication for doing it. It is also the expression of both polarities, making it a complete and whole expression of the dual-nature of self. To paraphrase Yogananda, by transcending the inhalation and exhalation of the breath we can find that which is whole and single. It's the unity of the Yin and the Yang, the Sun and the Moon, the light and the dark in all of us. The moment you divide reality you cannot embrace it. When you create duality, you cannot embrace the one reality. Popular methods of breath control include the 14 Yoga breaths and the seemingly inspired Wim Hoff method and others of today.

Purging

On beginning our journey into breath training we must first crete awareness of our breathing. This is as simple as sitting quietly and still to monitor our own breathing patterns and their effects. We might notice some imbalances or difficulties, we may notice pains or irregular timings. When we begin to sense these subtle dysfunctions, we can turn our concentration towards destroying any previous concepts and limitations we hold around breathing, in order to release what is no longer needed and begin setting new patterns. We could look at this as removing impurities from our breathing apparatus which includes not just the lungs but the diaphragm, chest and rib muscles, trachea and so on. We can also use the cleansing methods of Shat Kriya for this, such as Neti (nostril cleansing with water).

Resetting

This stage takes the form of neutralising the breath through breath balancing techniques such as Ujjayi breath, where you would take a long, slow inhalation followed by a controlled, slow exhalation while making the sound of an ocean wave with your throat. Neutralising the airways also means to equalise the effort coming from each lung and nostril, using Nadi Shodhana (alternate nostril breathing for energy pathway cleansing) and Anulom Vilam (alternate nostril breathing for airway cleansing). There is of course no substitute for learning these kinds of techniques live in person with someone, but there are also many online tutorials you can find for these techniques to follow along with.

Initiation

Being initiated into breathing practice is quite different from other skills, since it's something most of us believe to be naturally good at. The process of beginning your intense research and finding a teacher is the rite of passage granted to us by knowledge. It is perfectly fine to teach oneself to breathe better through online learning and slow, steady practice. However, for Kriya Yoga in particular it is most important that you seek a qualified teacher to initiate you. This is because Kriya Yoga is not just a casual breathing practice that you do when you feel like it, such as before or after a workout, or once in the morning - it is an intense daily practice which requires much dedication. For perspective, a beginner Kriya yogi may employ his technique 14-28 times a day. Indeed, this is why Yogananda named it "the aeroplane route".

Developing
Progressing forwards from our initiation, we can start to work on basic breathing techniques of pranayama such as *Kapalbhati* (heating breath or manual hyperventilation). These techniques are not styles of breathing we are used to using on a daily basis, if at all. They are almost like secret techniques the body holds and brings out in times of extreme stress or difficulty in order to help us keep going and stay alive. The ancient yogis realised that if we manually perform the natural breathing reactions our body has to extremities, we can directly control other functions of the body which we cannot normally manage with the brain, including nervous system activation or pacification, heart rate adaptation, homeostasis and hormonal balancing. Moving on to the advanced practices organically and at a rate appropriate for your level is how we can come to gain much more control over how our body is functioning in all scenarios.

Integrating
At this stage we will be proficient in using a variety of breathing patterns and merging them with different activities to reap the benefits. We become sensitive to the effects of different combinations where we play with timing and technique, learning the use of those breaths and coming to understand breath itself as a deeper, tangible concept. It is here where we really begin to access the true spiritual relationship between the breath, consciousness and cosmic energy.

Expressing
Having learnt a wide variety of techniques, we can finally use breathing a method of expression. Expressing your energy and spirit into your breath is how we make the whole process personal to us. A good example of this is singing, which requires excellent breath control alongside other things. Another is playing the didgeridoo, a wind instrument native to Australia. It is played by pushing air from the mouth into the long wooden tube with high pressure, producing a deep and continuous drone sound. In order to play this instrument a special breathing technique called circular breathing is employed, whereby the musician inhales through the nose without stopping the flow of air coming out of the mouth. I was taught a technique for learning circular breathing in India, by a friend I met who plays the didgeridoo. He told me to blow bubbles into a cup of water through a straw and practice inhaling through my nose without stopping the bubbles.

Fusing
Finally by becoming one with the breath and knowing how to use it in all aspects of life, we gain a tool which is primal in its basis yet so much more powerful than we could have imagined. A Master of your own breath, never again the victim of your own unconscious breathing, but now the holder of a powerful technique which has brought you towards an enhanced sense of self-awareness, peace and the bliss of Samadhi.

HEALING PATH

PATH	TYPE	POLARITY	SCIENCE	YOGA	PRIMARY BRAIN REGIONS
Healing	Body	–	Rehabilitation, Therapy	Yin Restorative, Ayurveda	Hypothalamus

SERIES A:

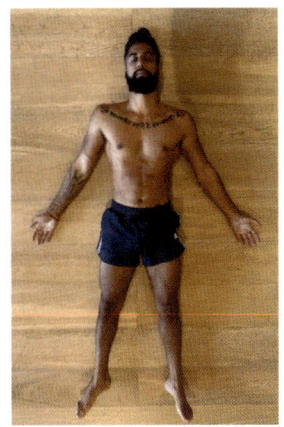

Shavasana (Corpse)

Supta Virasana (Reclining Hero)

Ustrasana (Camel)

SERIES B:

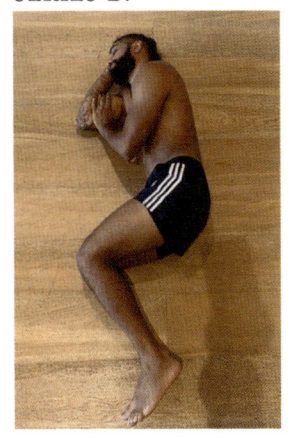

Parsva Shavasana (Side Corpse)

Balasana (Child)

Uttana Shishosana (Puppy)

SERIES A: Beginning with *Shavasana*, we learn complete bodily relaxation with the feet turned out and palms up in order to receive the cosmic healing currents. *Supta Virasana* creates greater opening of the heart, core and sacral centres whilst remaining passive on the floor. *Ustrasana* is a similar position but is not passive, it requires the addition of strength and active alignment.

SERIES B: *Parsva Shavasana* is also known as the recovery position. Rolling to the right elevates the heart above the body and thus reduces pressure on the heart muscles. Rolling to the left helps digestion and sleep by keeping the flow of stomach fluids towards the intestines instead of back up the esophagus. *Balasana* gives a secure, grounded feeling whilst pressing the forehead onto the floor stimulates the vagus nerve, which helps us relax and release stress. *Uttana Shisosana* is a more active version of the passive Balasana, where the head looks forward and effort is concentrated into the stretch to release compression of the spine.

> *"The fully matured man has no fear, no defense; he is psychologically completely open and vulnerable"* – **Osho**

If someone were to experience intense feedback from the senses through physical injury or trauma, it might scramble the brain and nervous system, leaving remnants of shock reverberating in the body and mind. This memory is what we know as trauma. The body carries several types of trauma – that of itself, injuries and learnt reactions. That of the mind's trauma – tight shoulders and headaches indicating mental stress. The trauma of the emotion – arms folded and hunched over, defensively protecting the heart from attack. In this way we can see that it is not just a choice but a necessity to employ the discipline of self-care, healing and self-love.

Psychological trauma however, is another ball game completely and requires an exceptionally deep level of self-inquiry. According to Jiddu Krishnamurti it is the sole cause of all dis-ease and illness. Krishnamurti (1895-1986) was an Indian philosopher who was deemed a child prodigy by the Theosophical Society who mentored him, who eventually became a leading figure of philosophy in the UK and USA. He is famous for positing that what we choose to pay attention to creates our experience, and that only.

He maintained until he died that we are not the multiple psychological identities (id, ego and superego), or any other conceptualised fragmentation of the mind. He would go on to say that by dividing the mind with thought, we automatically create a conflict of identity - the same thing we do when we identify ourselves too much with another person (dependency), a country (nationalism), an emotion, the ego, or any other attachment which we hold ourselves dependent on, even a belief in God. His mantra was that whatever thoughts we choose to give our attention to governs the state of our mind and our experience.

By fluctuating between or discussing any other temporary identities or dependencies, we create conflict between what we are and what we want to be, and that is not the peace and oneness of self that we seek. He maintained that in order to move past trauma to non-trauma, we cannot leave the trauma intact and escape it - we must dissolve it. That trauma cannot ever truly be swept under some psychological rug, supressed or escaped, only dissolved.

Krishnamurti believed that God was created by humans, by thought - that the attributes we ascribe to God are all of the things we think of as the highest virtues of existence. Therefore he surmises that God is actually just a result of thought, worshipping its own idea of what is virtuous and good, meaning that this virtue and goodness must originate in us. Paying attention to that aspect of ourselves, or God, is simply then to remind ourselves of that good nature in us and strive towards it.

Logo of the Theosophical Society; in the middle, the Ankh - man and his environment in constant exchange. Around him, the 6-pointed star which represents all universal manifestation. Surrounding them both, the snake of cosmic energy, which is eating the Swastika (representing the wheel of time). Crowning the loop of time is the symbol Aum, the omnipotent sound which permeates all life and connects us to that which is not of this universe, the cosmic source of consciousness, God.

How does healing oneself lead to Samadhi? Well, let's take the example of looking after one's diet. I haven't eaten meat for 10 years on the date of writing this book, even though I grew up eating meat until I was 25. I can see that it is not "unnatural" to eat meat, since if you lived in Alaska for example you would have to catch fish to survive, you can't grow sufficient agriculture on ice. So I do believe that it is a part of natural cycles that animals eat other animals, and thus humans can too if they choose to. However, I personally took the decision not to after watching some eye opening documentaries, because I didn't want any of the physical gains I was making to be on the back of another being's suffering, because I resonate with animals so much – I can see the soul in their eyes. My friend told me at the time of writing this book that he had started veganism for his health, but soon realised he felt proud and happier knowing he was also saving animals. It's a beautiful example of how a person took on the task of self-care, and learn compassion and a deeper level of perception into his life just by following the process. Sadhguru says that to eat an animal which has emotion is to take on that emotion and energy, or that karma. The Brahmacharya (scripture for the rules of monkhood) says that the eating of meat is allowed under certain survival conditions, but that "abstention brings great reward." This is yet another example of the open and non-divisive nature of the Yogic way of life, where there is less judgement on actions and more critical thinking employed about circumstance and spiritual wisdom.

Purging
The purging of trauma from the body is incredibly complex and multi-faceted. This is why the health industry has a huge variety of specialists for all areas of the body – it would be considered wise to seek a doctor or therapist for many issues, unless one is qualified to assess and treat oneself. Useful and scientifically verified techniques for detoxifying and healing the body are pranayama (breath control), varying the diet, intermittent fasting methods, reducing intake of complex energy sources (animal product) and certain herbal medicines. We need to create space in the body for healing. The body is in a continual state of absorbing nutrients from the bloodstream into the cells and tissues, whilst also releasing toxins from the cells and tissues into the bloodstream. The balance and flow of nutrients is biased towards going into the tissues and cells, since we are constantly digesting food and liquids. When we detox or fast, we give the body a break from this continual process of digestion, which allows the blood to become clear of nutrients – this actually helps the body to release more toxic materials back into the blood, which can then be excreted. This is what we know as detoxification.

Resetting
Here we are focused on bringing the body to a space of relaxation, so that the nervous system's reflexes are calmed and we can begin to work on healing. Nervous twitches, jaw clenching, shoulder hunching and arm crossing are all signs and symptoms of holding energetic tension. So we must begin to understand that there is a great deal we can do ourselves to heal by just becoming still and letting go of the tight grip we have on life. To hold life gently, rather than clutch at it and squeeze it to death. We

also must become aware and accepting of the fact that abstinence of any habits that gave us dis-ease in the first place is a good idea.

Initiation
Beginning the process of rehabilitation, whether physical or diet based, is starting the process of self-care. Seeking the knowledge of a nutrition expert would be a good idea if you struggle with the complexities of food science, or seeking out a manual therapist for physical pains or dysfunctions which you don't know how to heal yourself. The key is that we set an intention here to do everything we can to remove our limiting pains and traumas, in order to move towards healing.

Developing
When we begin to understand the application of the therapies we go through, we can begin to learn the art of self-healing. This includes utilising all the forms of therapy and advice received before, but now also learning the methods and systems to do a large amount of that healing by and for yourself - for instance trigger point release with a massage ball and stretching techniques for tight muscles, or eating habits and food types which balance your digestive health. It is imperative that we learn what works for us as individuals by experimenting and keeping track of our progress as we develop.

Integrating
This is a stage where you are perhaps prepping your meals, or getting regular massages and stretching daily. Whatever it is that you need for your function and lifestyle, you have to stick with it and advance, you cannot stay still. The body must evolve or else it stagnates and that is when we get dis-ease. Integrating healing knowledge into our lives is not just to heal oneself, but to then move into higher levels of compassion and show others how they can heal, using techniques that you have explored and verified for yourself.

Expressing
Expressing oneself through healing can be a hard concept to grasp, but could be understood through examples such as ecstatic dance, Tai Chi, stretching/Yoga to music, or even just crying and letting it out. It's where you bring your whole being to the process of healing and begin to move on past that trauma. Maybe we have issues of self-doubt, or we are worried what people think of us when we dance. Maybe we feel tense all the time and need a gentle, flowing art to help us soften up. This is the process of connecting to the sensitive side of the soul and letting it speak through our thoughts, movements and energies.

Fusing
Many people find themselves feeling more than just a physical release when receiving a massage, or experience a deeper enjoyment in quenching their thirst on a hot day with cool water. There are other experiences of life we can gain access to depending on how well we look after ourselves. When we learn the rites of self-care, self-healing and self-love, we are no longer reliant on others to help us feel content and relaxed, we do not carry the tension of our past nor of the future, we are here and now, in Samadhi. From this compassion to self, arises compassion for others, which leads to peace.

MOVEMENT PATH

PATH	TYPE	POLARITY	SCIENCE	YOGA	PRIMARY BRAIN REGIONS
Movement	Body	+	Exercise, Sport	Hatha, Vinyasa	Frontal lobes, Cerebellum

SERIES A:

Malasana (Garland)

Eka Pada Malasana (One-legged Garland)

Skandasana (Warrior Squat)

SERIES B:

Uttanasana A (Forward Fold A)

Uttanasana B (Forward Fold B)

Virabhadrasana 3 (Warrior 3)

SERIES A: Starting with an absolute necessity for healthy hip function and related organ health, *Malasana* is the deep squat known and used all over the world as a resting or lifting position. We can practice *Eka Pada Malasana* to increase the difficulty and finally reach *Skandasana* which helps develop the hips for many other sporting applications.

SERIES B: *Uttanasana A* is a fascial stretch for the entire posterior chain which reverses the impact of long periods of sitting or immobilisation – it can be performed with slightly bent knees, drawing the navel toward the thighs. *Uttanasana B* requires anterior-pelvic tilt and straight lines through the body, increasing the intensity on the hamstrings and calves. *Virabhadrasana 3* moves onto one leg with the arms overhead, significantly increasing the strength and balance requirement.

Athleticism and Asceticism are one and the same. Just as an ascetic is devoted to his cause, so is an athlete. An ascetic brings his mind and senses under control and is devoted to realising God, or the singularity of all consciousness. Similarly, an athlete realises the same through the control of their strength. They who practice rhythmic and extreme movements, strengthening the hands and legs, obtain the knowledge of our body, which leads to self-awareness, which leads to peace. Enlightenment however is not found through unconscious mastery of 1000 yoga postures, or even of 1. It is simply having an awareness of the invisible string which connects your movement to that of the natural flows and cycles of the cosmos, making it an easy way to develop understanding of the body and thus yourself.

This Path has given me the most benefit in my 28 years of training, yet still not everything. It is one of the most difficult Paths – to realise oneself through the body, which is actually a temporary vessel for the soul and therefore not us at all. It is transient and impermanent, since no human body has ever cheated death. Your body is not the same now as it was when you were born, yet you were and are still *you*. So why do so many of us feel drawn towards this Path if it's so difficult? Well firstly, we are programmed by nature to move – our health is actually based on the continual "greasing" of our joints and organs and internal processes, indicated by the concept of mechanotransduction. When these things are functioning well, the body is in good health, but if we don't keep the wheels greased we run into dis-ease and dysfunction.

Take the sport of calisthenics for example – you can train in that Yang (active) discipline for many years without expressing the opposite polarity of that type of training (passive) which would include activities like stretching and manual therapy. You would surely end up with injuries and dysfunctions before long because your body has not been corrected for any faulty habits or patterns picked up and it has not been maintained or taken care of well enough.

Then we can look at the way that people fight in martial arts. The defensive nature of the arts are expressed as contraction and compression. It is to block, absorb and contain the opponent's energy until it becomes inert through control or submission. The opposite expression in fighting is expansion and explosion, where the martial artist "flings" himself at the opponent to create striking attacks. And so the balance of both expressions leads us to what we call mixed martial arts. There are of course other layers to the spectrum of attack and defense – there are counterattacks, feints and rhythm throwing which deepen the understanding of range and timing, leading to levels of observation above the average eye, fight science. Of course, it is wholly advised to have multiple coaches or teachers on this Path, since it is often the study of a lifetime for people to master just one art.

Purging
So to begin on this Path we must first destroy all of our weaknesses, which may hold us back from progression. In this context I am referring

to the forgetting and removal of unwanted habits and patterns in the body. A lot of this has to do with Path 2, Healing - but it is also possible to override or at least support the overriding of many dysfunctions purely through practice of the correct function.

Resetting
Resetting the body first requires learning how to articulate oneself into neutral postures, meaning those where we are symmetrical, equal and balanced such as standing straight or laying down. This helps us to ensure we have removed sufficient trauma and dysfunction so as not to disturb the balance of the body when attempting and learning new skills. Once further into this process we can look at correcting and equalising functional patterns such as the Squat, Deadlift, walking gait and general joint positioning across a variety of symmetry based movements.

Initiation
Taking the pledge to learn a new discipline, we move forward into our chosen discipline/s. Learning multiple physical disciplines at once is not recommended, whereas taking on other Paths is. Other physical disciplines create a pull of energy and concentration in different directions. To learn a physical skill we must become wholly engrossed in the art because we are training the nervous system to learn new patterns whilst possibly also simultaneously still purging old ones. If we confuse the nervous system with too many varying patterns, it won't keep any of them. It is generally therefore better to learn multiple physical disciplines over the course of years in an organic and natural order, perhaps overlapping, but not all at once.

Developing
Once we have practiced any individual physical art for a number of years, we begin to gain proficiency in the basic techniques. We become the "Senior student". Here we are learning advanced techniques and perhaps researching into picking up another new physical discipline to learn concurrently.

Integrating

Now we are bringing together all of what we have learnt into a systematic use of the techniques. This would be called getting your black belt in some martial arts, or in the army earning your stripes. It is the graduation of the student to a master of the fundamental techniques. This can only usually happen through a qualified guru or coach who recognises you as a master of the basics, but in the absence of one you can only compare and test yourself against the general standard for where you think your skill level is at. That can also be a good indicator of progress, like grades in school exams are given to a bell curve. But I would also assert that comparison is not what makes us complete. It is only self-development and progress that matters in the end. We just can't be claiming all sorts of expertise unless we can stand the test of time and competition.

Expressing

Here the practitioner begins to seed his own ideas and inspiration into his use of the techniques, and produces adaptations to suit them and their students. Finding expression of self in the flow of technique, a new style is born, your own unique style of that art.

Fusing

Now walking through life, as a master of a physical art, the practitioner has strengthened the body and come to know it for all it can be in that form of expression. He or she can finally taste competence, and a strong self-respect. When performing their art the master is absorbed and at one with their true nature in Samadhi, blissful in the state of effortless flow. If this seeking is continued with the constant learning of new arts, the body can eventually become fit for the expression of the higher consciousness and cosmos, the performance of the skill then becoming an act of bringing heaven down to Earth.

ASTRAL PATH

PATH	TYPE	POLARITY	SCIENCE	YOGA	PRIMARY BRAIN REGIONS
Astral	Mind	–	Meditation, Absorption	Dhyana, Samadhi	Amygdala, Pineal gland

SERIES A:

Sukhasana (Easy)

Ardha Padmasana (Half Lotus)

Padmasana (Full Lotus)

SERIES B:

Agnistambhasana (Fire Log)

Janu Sirsana (Head to Knee)

Dandasana (Staff)

SERIES A: *Sukhasana* is called "Easy posture" for a reason – it reduces the tension in the spine when sitting and makes it easy for us to cross our legs. It does however create tension in the hip adductors and flexors, leading us towards the practice of *Ardha Padmasana* which does the opposite and stretches those muscles. Finally, having achieved that on both sides, we can practice the iconic jewel of yoga *Padmasana*. Sitting this way keep the hips completely open and the triangle shape formed underneath the body provides a strong base for stability. Padmasana helps shift our bodyweight from the bottom of the spine towards the knees when seated, reducing spinal compression and any soreness of the glutes/ lower back which might develop from sitting for extended periods.

SERIES B: *Agnistambhasana* is an alternative sitting position which creates a square base underneath the legs rather than a triangle. Moving between different sitting postures can be important as the joints can begin to ache if left in any one position too long. *Janu Sirasana* is a great intermediary position and also helps prepare us for *Dandasana*, an upright position which helps channel kundalini up the spine towards the higher chakras.

The concept of meditation is a conundrum for many people. It requires a certain level of philosophical self-inquiry even just to understand why one might want to do it. But as our society becomes more awakened to the benefits through more accounts of success with it, meditation has become a concept now understood in the West.

More apt then is the question, how does one go about releasing (-) the mind through meditating? There are other disciplines here that can also be researched and experimented with, including astral projection, conscious dreaming and more. These are practices whereby you learn to become in active control of your experiences in your dream state, or going further, being able to experience your light body projected from your actual body.

"The real voyage of discovery consists, not in seeking new landscapes, but in having new eyes." – **Marcel Proust, 'La Prisonnière', the fifth volume of 'In Search of Lost Time'**

You see when you look at something, light reflects off of the object into your eye (reflection no.1). It then enters your eye through the lens and reflects onto the back of your eye (reflection no.2). This light is then converted to electrical signal by the optic nerve (energy format conversion). The brain then interprets that signal as what you are seeing. That's how our vision works – quite a series of steps and conversions before an image is actually processed. The bones of the forehead however are porous, meaning there a small micro holes in the bone. This allows light to pass directly through the forehead, which is then sensed and interpreted without any filter by the pineal gland, which has been referred to by many as "the seat of the Soul". This is why you can sense light with your eyes closed. To close and then turn the eyes up together is to look at the light through your "third eye", it is to see light without any distortion or reflection.

Purging
As Yogananda said, there can be more than 50,000 thoughts and sub-thoughts which occur in the average lifetime of 60 years. These thoughts, although useful for knowledge, also keep us in the state of temporary illusion, because by thinking we are fixating on that which is of this world. We can try many types of assisted meditation at this stage, which are aimed at kickstarting the process. These include therapies and other mind relaxing treatments. A good way to do this subconsciously is to listen to recorded affirmations before sleep or just on waking up, since they download straight into the subconscious that way due to the theta brain wave state.

Resetting
In this sense we must now reset our posture and our mind for meditation.

This will include some minimal work of Hatha Yoga asana, the 12 postures recommended by Patanjali in the Yoga Sutras. These are to enable us to sit longer without the body distracting us with discomfort. Any other discipline which aids mobilisation of the body whilst creating mental space through stillness is also fine. When we can bring ourselves to stillness, we are ready to be initiated.

Initiation
Again, the guide of a guru or coach is recommended here. They can help you navigate the complex levels of psychology that you have and through the numerous voices in your head which aspire to reason and feeling. Managing the maze which is the human mind is incredibly difficult, especially if the mind attempting to understand itself has flawed understandings or conceptions. A non-biased, non-partisan professional looking from the outside in can be so important for helping you to work through things you otherwise don't have the capacity to help yourself with.

Developing
Here the aim is to develop Dharana (concentration), to focus the mind on a set of thoughts or line of enquiry and to not deviate from this for a set period of time. In this we develop unwavering thought. It's a funny fact of life that we are plagued by those thoughts we don't wish to have, yet always forget those thoughts we wish to retain forever. However, that is the nature of this existence and in accepting that we can develop a new set of rules for how we choose to think. Common practices which can help us learn concentration include the *Trataka* fire gazing meditation and *Pranayama*, where the breath becomes the object of focus.

Integrating
Here we learn the role of observer, where we interpret our own thoughts or actions with some sense of higher judgement and reasoning. We are learning to unite that concept of infinite self with that of transient self,

or this body in this life. Observing oneself can be as simple as just sitting down to really feel and resonate with the meanings of our previous thoughts and actions in life. The purpose is not to wallow here in self-pity, regret or guilt. It is to understand our reactions to those situations and in time learn how, why and where they originated from within us.

Expressing
Having learnt how to be still and enter the alternative mind-state of observer, we begin to learn the process of observing without evaluating. The mind, monitoring its own thinking, learns to stop thinking about its own thinking. Then it becomes truly free of the trap that is continuous thought. We are observing the thought/s, but not reacting to them. It is a cocoon of invincibility to the 5 senses and external conditions. Unaffected by transient feelings the mind simply watches, not identifying itself with anything and reserving analysis or judgement for another time. It is in a way, trying to be the most impartial that you can be with yourself.

Fusing
Once we have practiced and become comfortable with entering that state of mind which is observing without thought, we have learnt the process of meditation. Here is the final key and salvation that we have worked for, for here we realise that through mediation, one can put the mind to rest at will by simply going into observation and absorption mode with the cosmos, each time bringing us home to a space where we can bask in the infinite stillness and unchanging bliss of Samadhi.

SCHOLAR PATH

PATH	TYPE	POLARITY	SCIENCE	YOGA	PRIMARY BRAIN REGIONS
Scholar	Mind	+	Concentration, Study of self	Dharana, Svadhyaya	Frontal lobes, Cerebral cortex

SERIES A:

Urdhva Hastasana (Upwards Salute)

Eka Pada Utkanasana (One-legged Chair)

Ardha Chakrasana (Half Wheel)

SERIES B:

Nirsanana (Headstand)

Padma Nirsanana (Lotus Headstand)

Adho Mukha Vrksasana (Handstand)

SERIES A: Pointing the hands towards the sky and focusing the dhrishti (yogic gaze), we can learn concentration through *Urdhva Hastasana*. By moving onto one leg with *Eka Pada Utkanasana*, we significantly increase the difficulty of balancing and must work harder to keep our gaze still. Looking upwards or in non-familiar directions can be disconcerting since it affects our balance, so by developing this multi-directional focus we can move towards better concentration skills, such as those required for the infamously difficult *Ardha Chakrasana*, where the head is upside down and looking backwards with the arms overhead.

SERIES B: Inverting the body activates the parasympathetic nervous system and helps circulate pooled blood in the legs back towards the heart. Beginning in *Nirsasana* we practice the art of relaxed but focused stillness. Being upside down allows us to learn postural strength and experience a different direction of sight, which makes balancing harder and enhances concentration. Moving to *Padma Nirsanana*, the addition of the lotus to the headstand makes the form and balancing act harder thus intensifying the practice. Finally we can learn *Adho Mukha Vrksasana* which creates a less stable base on the hands instead of the head, forcing us to take control and articulate minute joint movements to create the straight line. The postural benefits and increased focus created by these positions enhances one's ability to concentrate even in conditions which are unfamiliar.

We have already been introduced to the concept of Dharana which is concentration. Now we will explore putting that concentration to use, on things which we can study that lead us to knowledge of the self. If you study something enough, you will merge with it and find traces of source consciousness or God in it. Studying sciences and arts helps us to further our own understanding of ourselves as well as the world around us, since the microcosm is also an expression of the macrocosm, and vice versa. It is called the Path of Focus because if intelligence is simply held by itself and there is no ability to attach it to anything of importance, it becomes useless. The intelligence is not the aim, the aim is to be able to remained focused on something no matter how difficult it is to understand, because this particular Path and goal can bring us to self-awareness, rather than hyper-awareness of the environment which is known as "book smarts".

"The intellect is like a knife – it dissects whatever it's used on into smaller understandable pieces. The identity is the hand that holds it. The hand that holds decides whether a knife will take or save a life. The knife does not decide. In the hands of a surgeon, it may save a life, in an irresponsible hand it takes a life. Depending on what kind of identity you have taken on, accordingly your intellect either becomes a fruitful thing for everyone around you, or it becomes a destructive process. Intellect is a useless instrument unless its fed with some data – if there is no data and we wipe out all your memory, suddenly you will look like a dumb person even though you have a sharp intellect, because intellect cannot function without data." – **Sadhguru Jaggi Vasudev**

Purging
In this Path we first need to remove any bias, dogmas and beliefs that we are holding which could obstruct our clarity of sight when learning. If we cannot do this, we are stuck in a non-evolving form of thought which cannot defend itself against inquiry, so it cannot be the truth unless it still stands after enquiry. I'm not saying to do away with morals and ethics, I'm saying to be able to bring those into question fairly and not to identify with them so much that they distort our vision and make us resistant to change and learning.

Resetting
Here, we relearn and form new understandings of the basic sciences and ways of life that were taught in school. We have to bring our level back to a place where we can move on from elementary levels of thought. We are

taught in school to think and remember what we are taught, but not to question what we are taught. This is a grave mistake - the very process of scepticism and probing is invaluable in relation to self-awareness - where the brilliant human brain can create all kinds of excuses and loopholes, being able to critique ideas through to the end allows us to gain strength in those ideas and accept them as deeper truths, or to discard them as non-truths if they are exposed as so. This can only happen through the process of inquiry.

Initiation
The process of self-inquiry through knowledge is referred to in the Vedas as *Svadhyaya*. We do not necessarily need a guru to help us ask existential questions, as most young children have shown us by asking how babies are made. Naturally inquisitive, we are curious by nature although we usually need someone to help us understand the answers. Initiation here is the point where we decide we want to learn about a subject or something in greater detail – to see the real truth behind how it works and what it means.

Developing
As a person develops intellectually, they begin to see the lines which join what to a novice would appear as completely disjointed cues. We can begin to connect subtle levels of knowledge with more overtly obvious forms, for example; if I told you that the Sun was a ball of fire in the sky, this is overtly obvious. If the Sun disappeared, the Earth and all its life would freeze in less than 48 hours, that is deeper knowledge. Deeper still, I could tell you that the Sun provides all light and that light is literally knowledge – this kind of reference to the Sun as representing knowledge is a more subtle level of understanding about how it interacts with our planet and us. Moving forward in academic studies of the world and self, the learner will come to a place of cognitive intelligence, where concepts begin to make more sense and the world lights up in colour before the eyes.

Integrating
With all this new information to light from the devoted practice of studying, the learner starts to connect theories and formulas together, like an eccentric theorist, seeing all the minute details and connecting points which bring the universe into such organisation. In this state he starts to feel the tingles and power of knowledge. Looking beyond the lines and dots, he starts seeing the shapes they make and how they compare or differ with other shapes and ideas.

Expressing
When the learner begins to express his knowledge in unique ways, it usually manifests as teaching. He moves toward restyling and representing information in a new light, one that has been fashioned from his own personal interpretation of the field but still holding to the core of the facts. Becoming a guru in your own right is the fruit of arriving at truth – when truth is uncovered there is nothing more joyful than to share it so that the entire cosmos can revel in it and benefit from the enlightenment.

Fusing
In the knowledge that he has become an expert who has thoroughly explored a particular topic, he is convinced he has merged with the subject of thought and knows it inside out. In this way, he recognises the representation of his own being and self inside the subject field, as well as that of the cosmos'. Resting at last, he is blissful in the truth that is unchanging and the unwavering nature of the self, Samadhi.

RHYTHM PATH

PATH	TYPE	POLARITY	SCIENCE	YOGA	PRIMARY BRAIN REGIONS
Rhythm	Emotion	–	Sound, Vibration	Mantra, Nada	Temporal lobes, Cerebellum

SERIES A:

Adho Mukha Svanasana (Downwards Facing Dog)

Tandavasana (Shiva's Cosmic Dance)

Gomukhasana (Cow Face)

SERIES B:

Urdhva Mukha Svanasana (Upwards Facing Dog)

Camatkarasana (Wild Heart)

Samakonasana (Equal Angle)

SERIES A: *Adho Mukha Svanasana* is a widely used and commonly known position today. Although it can be made to be intense, however it is often referred to as a "resting posture". This is because it serves as a base position or intermediary between other positions in general yoga flows such as Surya Namaskar (Sun Salutation). It helps prepare the body for work and activate the posterior chain. *Tandavasana* is relatively easy looking but is not – it creates a rotational torque in the spine whilst demanding posterior chain activation, giving us another dimension of expression for our spinal energies. *Gomukhasana* is the bane of many yoga practitioners due to its difficulty and awkwardness, but gives us advanced hip rotation for floor based movement. It is actually the default position for playing the Sitar, an ancient Indian instrument popularised across the world by legendary musician Pandit Ravi Shankar.

SERIES B: *Urdhva Mukha Svanasana* is in some ways the counterpart to Adho Mukha Svanasana. When a person moves back and forth between the two positions with rhythm, the movement is called a *Dand* or *Hindu Push-up*. It is used the world over in sports including martial arts, Crossfit and performing arts. *Camatkarasana* can be translated as "the ecstatic unfolding of the enraptured heart". It allows our body to gracefully twist and turn whilst helping us release expression from the heart and sacral plexuses. The dancer's split, otherwise known as *Samakonasana*, teaches us the full range of our open hip capsules - the more we can expand and extend our body into the surrounding space, the further we can broadcast our feelings and energy into that space.

It is said in the Natya Sashtra (Hindu treatise on performing arts, 500BCE);

> *"The primary function of the performing arts is not entertainment. The primary function of the performing arts is to transport the individual in the audience into a parallel dimension, where they are forced to question their own abilities, beliefs and morals."*

The use of music and sound has been popular through the ages and is timeless, simply because of its ability to bring us into either a space of complete movement or stillness. In that moment we relax our very being, we release (-) our emotions through our expression of sound and movement. The rhythm in which we move is foundational to our experience of how it feels, and it is how the audience interprets our energy through movements and sounds. It sets the pace of our emotion.

AUM is the ancient Vedic equivalent of Amen to the Christians, Amin to the Muslims and Om to the Tibetans. It is the first Word of God, which is God, as referred to in the Old Testament. The letters are the only sounds that you can make without inflictions of the teeth and tongue, A U M, representing creation, perseverance and dissolution, respectively. There is another sound attributed to AUM, which is called Turiya. It could be represented like this _, because its meaning is "unutterable sound". It is the end of the cycle, and the beginning of the next one. It is the space that holds the reverberance of the cycle of creation before it, a moment of stillness before the repeat and beginning of a new one. This Mantra alone has the power to bring you to absolute stillness and self-awareness, since it is the sound of the entire Universe. Yogananda says that the practising Yogi soon starts to hear the sound of AUM in all they do. Mantra are powerful sounds which are chanted in set tones and orders to neutralise or amplify certain vibrations within us. When listened to they are extremely powerful, but when chanted the vibration is created deep inside with the emotion of the soul, enabling true release (-) through expression. All that is needed for this body, is to know how to use it properly, to know how to maintain, tune and masterfully care for it, to play it in all its fullness like the magnificent instrument that it is. Nada Yoga and Mantra Yoga are to be engrossed in the study and practice of this natural rhythm and all its permutations.

Purging
Vibration is not an easy thing to clear. It is the very substance of our formation, it is what is holding all the atoms we are made of together. How to undo such a force? My recommendation here is that we start by shaking, vigorously shaking the body and loosening the muscles and joints, relieving any prior tension. Learning to remove the superego from the equation, which is what you think other people think of you. To dance like no-one is watching.

Resetting
When we have done sufficient work to remove the ego and superego's concerns from the process, we must come to know silence and stillness again, but this time as a representation of sound. As Turiya, the unutterable sound. We begin to listen to the sound of that sound, which is the sound of silence.

Initiation
Noticing that silence actually has a sound, we can hear AUM in it. The gentle "whir of the vibratory motor", as Yogananda calls it. We can move onto listening to set frequencies, such as the healing frequency of the Earth 432Hz, the Schumann resonance at 7.83Hz, or even those frequencies which match the chakras, to help us to find a template for vibration and rhythm that we can follow.

Developing
At this point you could either self-learn or take a Guru or a Teacher to help you learn to start making sounds and vibrations. This could take the form of learning a musical instrument, learning mantras, singing, producing music, dancing to music or simply listening to music.

Integrating
As this is another extremely complex and expansive Path, it is really useful

to get at least some guidance, but vibration is so powerful that generally I believe when we are working with the frequencies that any level of competence can have profound effects on the self. Here we learn how to pull together all of our learnings around rhythm, pace, melody and harmony in order to create a seemingly ordered set of vibrations that have specific effect and purpose.

Expressing
The stage that everybody wants to be at, especially with music, since it is such a pure expression of emotion. We cannot reach here until we have sufficient understanding of vibration as a whole. Even the words you use are powerful because they are sounds, they have meanings, deeply loaded with power. That is why we call it spelling, because words are spells. Once we understand that power, we can begin to express ourselves through that language of vibration and the evolved form, which we call music.

Fusing
Using the rhythm and understanding of vibration has huge implications for how we set our own patterns, how we might disturb other people's patterns, and how we interact with the patterns and natural cycles of the universe. Interacting with the universe means to observe moments of the day where the energy changes, for instance at sunrise and sunset, twilight times of day where the light and dark hang in precarious balance and there is not quite one or the other. This is a transformative time of day not to be wasted. Becoming not just aware but synced with nature's and one's own rhythms, the learner is filled with the joy of full expression of self and the cosmos, in Samadhi.

TANTRIC PATH

PATH	TYPE	POLARITY	SCIENCE	YOGA	PRIMARY BRAIN REGIONS
Tantric	Emotion	+	Self-control, Connection	Kundalini, Tantra	Amygdala, Pineal gland

SERIES A:

Setu Bandhasana (Bridge)

Eka Pada Setu Bandhasana (One-Legged Bridge)

Chakrasana (Wheel)

SERIES B:

Chaturanga Dandasana (Four-Limbed Staff)

Bakasana (Crane)

Planche (Gymnastic)

SERIES A: By practicing *Setu Bandhasana* we gain hip extension, core control and leg strength. This is hugely important for raising kundalini – to do this we need to tuck the sacrum underneath the hips (posterior pelvic tilt), whilst squeezing the perineal muscles which drive energy up the spine and also block energy from dropping out the other way. *Eka Pada Setu Bandhasana* is the natural progression from this where we move to one leg, increasing the control requirement for the core and upright leg. Ending in *Chakrasana* we create full extension and activation of the spinal discs and energies.

SERIES B: Starting with the fundamental strength base of *Chaturanga Dandasana* will help us move onto learning arm-balance postures which demand higher volumes of concentration, technique and energy. The sacrum still tucked under to activate kundalini, we can slowly move from practising the well-known *Bakasana* variations towards achieving the rarer *Planche*, an elite gymnastic position most known for its illusion of levitation and incredible difficulty. Due to the extreme strength requirement and unusual biomechanical structure of the position, it is known to take at least one year to achieve, assuming a proficient fitness history and dedicated daily practice.

Kundalini is extremely advanced and its authentic teachers are very rare today. It's the most potent way to do it, but it will demand a certain dimension of discipline and focus which a regular life in society will not allow. This is why it is usually reserved as a practice for monks in the form of *tantra*. Tantra has unfortunately become another misnomer of understanding in the West, much like the term Yoga in general. Tantra literally pertains to the study of energy management. The Kama Sutra, a subtext of the Tantric discipline, is not simply a book of sex positions. It is in actuality "A treatise on the fulfilment of sexual and emotional needs, of both self and the significant-other". The Kama Sutra was given to humanity in order to help us fulfil those needs in a fruitful way, rather than just wasting or tainting our energies with fruitless activities. The way of celibacy was also prescribed for monks in the Vedic texts, as an alternative method to avoid this. The two dualistic viewpoints come from the "Right hand" or "White" path and the "Left hand" or "Red" path of Tantra.

Tantra was a set of disciplines given on the basis of whether one was to become a monk or not (surely the aeroplane route to self-awareness, but not for everyone). For those who would not practice celibacy and abstinences, for those who wanted to get married and reproduce etc., the Left hand path was given, which Kama Sutra falls under.

According to Medical Science, only the best blood tissue (marrow) is used to provide the nutrients for sperm cells, which originate in the testes. Scientists believe that 32kg of food produces 800g of blood which eventually produces 20g of semen, the whole process taking around 72 days. More than 20g can be expelled in just one ejaculation. How precious this fluid is!

> **It is said in the Vedas;** *"Forty meals make a drop of blood, 40 drops of blood make a drop of bone marrow, 40 drops of bone marrow make a drop of semen, the elixir of life." (1500BC)*

For this reason, Ayurveda, the Indian science of medicine extolls *brahmacharya* (the practice of celibacy) for its exceptional health benefits, in context for monks wishing to take the aeroplane route. Those who waste their semen become unsteady and agitated. They lose their physical and mental energy, and weaken their memory, mind, and intellect. The practice of either celibacy or injaculation (Tantric method of withholding semen when having sex) leads to a boost of bodily energy, clarity of intellect, gigantic will power, retentive memory, and a keen spiritual intellect. It creates a sparkle in the eyes and a luster on the cheeks. Emotion is simply energy in motion, e-motion, which can be activated (+) by taking the Path of Tantra.

Purging
Staring the Path of Tantra is difficult - we must first start by clearing away energies from within ourselves that are not conducive to our health. This can take the form of many other therapies already listed. It is important to understand here that when dealing directly with the energy system we have to be careful of who and what we let into our personal space and energies.

Resetting
Having cleared the stagnant or unstable energies of ourselves and other people in our lives who are bringing that unwanted energy, we take the step of being neutral. That is, learning how not to be extreme in our behaviours and habits, to learn self-control and abstinence where necessary to maintain good health of our energy body.

Initiation
To be initiated into Right hand Tantra is a slow process requiring ordainment into monkhood. It is to become so dedicated to this Path that you will sacrifice and surrender your role in society. To learn tantra but still remain in society is also possible by studying the Left hand Tantra, which gives detail on the methods and disciplines around managing the energy system for those who will still engage in a "material life". This managing of our energies and understanding of how it interconnects us is invaluable and we are all capable of learning that over time.

Developing
As we begin to learn more ways of activating and containing our energies, we will find that our mannerisms and character become more balanced. The mind, body and emotion will all come together at ease, as the energy body begins to vibrate at a more harmonious frequency. Our perception changes and we are more sensitive to energies and patterns. We realise that anything we do to disrupt or violate the harmony of the electromagnetic field (internal or external), is in fact at odds with nature – realising this

we can develop a better sense of how to behave and act. A great practice I was once taught for this is the silent approach. When you wake up in the morning you can spend the first 15 minutes doing everything you would normally, but trying not to make a single sound. Placing a cup of tea down gently, walking without stomping down the stairs, etc. I found this to be a wonderful method for becoming more sensitive to the impact of our energies on everything within and around.

Integrating
The third eye Ajna opens and reveals the sixth sense, then we are able to direct energy at will, either through broadcasting our feelings far and wide or being more receptive to the conscious and unconscious expressions of energy from all other beings including human and others. Learning how to maximise or subdue our energetic expression gives us full control of what we put out into the shared electro-magnetic environment.

Expressing
The soul and emotion then find expression through the energy. We can send intention at will, produce willpower from deep inside at will and focus our energies into our tasks at will. This is where the true loving nature and shining attributes of humankind begin to show through the cracks of the body. We must live in harmony and accordance with the rules of nature and consciousness in order to find the true peace we are looking for.

Fusing
Unable to contain the infinite amounts of light energy pouring into him from the cosmos, the Tantra practitioner develops an aura of light around him, seemingly bursting at the seams with pure energy. He is absorbed in the joy of a thousand suns, the opposite of "blacking out" or going unconscious, he "whites out" and becomes fully conscious, into the state of unchanging and everlasting bliss, which is known as Samadhi.

CHAPTER 6
Gurus, Coaches, Disciples & Students

"Until you make the unconscious conscious, it will direct your life, and you will call it fate." – **Carl Jung, Psychologist**

"The Guru does not bring about Self-realisation. He simply removes all the obstacles to it. The Self is always realized."
– **Sri Ramana Maharshi, Indian Sage/Scholar**

We've gone into a fair amount of detail on a variety of practices and for most I have recommended the seeking of a guru or teacher for certain aspects of learning. I want to start this chapter by expanding on the concepts of gurus and coaches alongside what it means to be a disciple or student.

As a child I was a fan of the Disney movie *Alice in Wonderland* based on writer Lewis Carroll's book of the same name. In it, there is a scene where Alice asks the hilariously profound Cheshire Cat which way she should go, for she is lost…

> Alice: *"Would you tell me please, which way I ought to go from here?"*
> *"That depends a good deal on where you want to get to,"* said the Cat.
> *"I don't much care where—"* said Alice.
> *"Then it doesn't matter which way you go,"* said the Cat.
> *"—so long as I get somewhere,"* Alice added as an explanation.
> *"Oh, you're sure to do that,"* said the Cat, *"if you only walk long enough".*

The Sanskrit words *Gu* and *Ru* put together literally mean "dispeller of darkness". A poetic explanation for a teacher or guide, who illuminates the path for those who are ignorant of the terrain thus far. It does not mean, how a lot of the West infer, "absolute expert who is enlightened in every aspect of life".

All people who have a child or have taught a child something, have been a guru to that person in the formative years of that person's life. But teaching a child who is an open template is easier than teaching an adult who has their own views, memory (karma) and resistance (trauma) built up over decades. These things require more than just the naturally learned behaviours we are endowed with for childcare such as protection and nurturing. They require an extended sense of understanding and also compassion which goes beyond those of just our relatives, in order to feel the altruistic desire to help someone who we are not related to.

I also want to bring attention to the fact that every guru is also a human being – for a person to step into that role, they have to separate their own nature from that which is being discussed. It's like stepping into a different persona temporarily, to speak of ideals and truth is the same as channelling and expressing things of a higher nature. When one is speaking the truth like that, in a way it is not that person speaking anymore – it is a higher consciousness speaking through them, they have become a vessel and conduit for truth while they are delivering it. When they are not engaged in the job and role of being a teacher, they go back to being themselves, which is fallible and human. Just like everybody else in the real world who has a work persona that is different to how they are outside of work.

Nobody demands that a school teacher who is raising our next generation should be a perfect human being and behave identically at work and at home. So why is it expected of a guru? It is because the most common (although shallow and basic) Western understanding of a guru is an "enlightened" bearded monk-like person who has completely renounced the material world, is overtly wise and has an infallible character. The notion goes further, where any Indian man who sits like that and chants Aum will be subjected to that character stereotype and be expected to live up to it. This is as far from the truth as could be – gurus are not monks, they are teachers of society and follow a very different set of ideals. Gurus are respected for their knowledge, monks for their piety. The monk finds truth and leaves society to bask in it – the guru finds truth and comes back to society to help everyone else see it – to me that is a far more noble cause than just saving oneself. This misunderstanding of who can call themselves a guru and what is expected of them needs to be cleared up.

One who has seen the light outside, compared to those still sitting in darkness just watching projected shadows (think Plato's Cave), is blessed indeed. The difference between a monk and a guru is, the monk stands up through his process of self-awareness, sees the bright light outside and goes to it. There he stays in the sun, enjoying all of its warmth and beauty. The guru however, goes outside and enjoys the sun, but then goes back inside to wake everybody else up and bring them outside. This is a completely compassionate and noble role in society, and in my opinion should be the role held in highest respect in society – the role of the teacher. Without teachers we are doomed as a race, for all knowledge would be lost, everybody would be illiterate and uneducated, and we would surely plunge back into the darkness from whence we came.

What is not fallible is truth, and if truth is spoken that illuminates your life, the source need not come into question here. Therefore it's important to realise that the emotional and personal life of a man or woman are to be separated from their role as a teacher. Those teachers who have been seen by society as infallible, both in their role as guru and in their personal life, are called saints – and I am no saint. But I am a teacher, and I step into that role as often as I can in order to help bring others to the light I have seen.

Manorama D'Alvia is one of the leading teachers in Sanskrit and Yoga Philosophy. And mentions that there has been a considerable amount of bad press when it comes to some Yoga or spiritual gurus over recent years – she states in an interview with Jacob Kyle that there are sometimes abuses of power in any relationship. "We must understand that the teacher is embodied knowledge, and that students must serve as a "Chatra" for the teachings. Chatra in Sanskrit means "umbrella" and refers to the practice of passing on to the world the sacred teachings of the guru while holding an umbrella over the negative, or perhaps more profane aspects of the human being. She clarifies that this is not intended to mean that the student should somehow block the truth, but rather that the spirit of the teachings should not be seen as being tarnished by the humanity of a particular guru."

In India's long and ancient traditions, there was only one type of student a guru would take and that is a *Shishya* (disciple). The meaning of the word disciple is apparent from its uses, such as the 12 Disciples of Christ. Therefore the original Guru-Shishya relationship is unlike most teacher-student relationships today. It would begin with the disciple approaching the guru for help. The disciple is only accepted and initiated after rigorous assessment by the guru who decides whether or not they are fit for the teachings. There have been many accounts of people turned away from gurus over the ages even though they begged for years to be taught.

The guru provides free teachings, lodging and food for the disciple – in return the disciple becomes an aid to the guru, helping with any tasks and chores. Both would hold that relationship in utmost sacredness, the guru's duty and purpose in life being only to pass on what he knows to his disciple. The disciple therefore eventually becomes not just a master and guru in his own right, but also the legacy and lineage of the guru.

What is being passed on is not about genetic or individual legacy, but simply the succession of truth in its infinite varied expressions.

Nowadays, no such relationship exists in the "standard teaching industry". There are periods were one might be a disciple in action, but nobody really takes on just one teacher for life. That is because we have come to understand a few things – firstly that we need multiple teachers to learn multiple things in this new age of information, secondly that no one man is an island to himself, and thirdly that people are usually just not dedicated enough to undergo such extreme conditions as to be a disciple. It means to sacrifice your whole life to that learning. To do whatever you are told by your guru without question, no matter how seemingly pointless, unrelated or inane.

Nowadays people want to have more control over their own lives and the things they do, so the role of disciple is becoming outdated. The guru's role still lives on however, but it must take on a different format to be relevant in today's society. Today, people are more relatable to what we would called a student rather than a disciple. A student is someone who receives the darshan (blessing) of a teacher's lessons, but in return gives dakshini (offering, or payment), in lieu of being taught. It is a trade for information.

Now some people are going around, guru to guru, teacher to teacher, asking for darshan everywhere. They believe that by paying for information from every possible source that they will end up with the "master file" and know everything, but this is almost the opposite to what actually happens - what you get that way is just a convoluted sack of mixed up and nuanced information from multiple sources, which you have to sift and sort through yourself to make any sense of. This is not how learning should occur – in school you are given one teacher for one subject for a reason. The substitute teacher can barely integrate themselves when they are called in because they are not in flow with the student's progress and history. So it is better to limit the amount of inputs we get by researching and seeking out the guru who is best for us in any subject field. Not just the one who knows the most, the one who can teach us best in the way we need to learn. Again that requires taking the time to do research and self-inquiry.

Quality of teaching is also an important thing for us to put value on – in this day and age we have allowed so many people to become famed as teachers and coaches who clearly shouldn't be. They have managed this through the leverage of social media and presenting themselves as something they are not, as well taking advantage of the continually lowered standards of entry into professional fields such as personal training, yoga teaching, therapy and more. You can become qualified as a personal trainer or yoga teacher in 4 weeks and online without ever having met your teacher – it makes no sense to me that a random person with no prior experience of anatomy, exercise, fitness or biology should be allowed to market themselves as an expert in teaching a movement science or a manual therapy. However the demands of capitalism and industrial forces deem that they are.

In that type of situation it is increasingly important that people research the disciplines they want to learn in order to find reputable coaches, not just being awed by edited photos on Instagram but by researching the person in front of them and the standard of coaching across the discipline. We must seek out not just capable teachers (everyone seems capable to a newbie), but reputable teachers who have earned their stripes. This way, we create a market where the highest truth is what is most valued, over the highest power of influence. In this way and only in this way can we move away from this era of fake gurus and unqualified teachers claiming more than they are, and move towards that which is real teaching, that which teaches truth and stands the test of time.

What make a teacher is not just capability. It is also knowledge of the art, experience of the art, and experience of teaching. Therefore to be impressed by something like a handstand for instance, when the teacher is not even in a straight line, and to become so awed by this flawed handstand that you offer this person money to teach you, is to be fooled by any old magic, by anyone, anywhere. You should at least take it upon yourself to know what you are looking at, or risk being taught how to also do something the wrong way.

The student, once finding a guru or teacher, must still observe the sacred qualities of being a student. Remembering that the student is fortunate enough to know such a teacher in person, whilst millions across the world have no access to such gifts, he is delighted in his guru's presence and offers utmost respect through a few things; dakshini (offering), compliance, dedication, respect and humility. If these things are not offered to the guru, or the student falls short of them, the guru can just tell you to get lost! And literally, just like that, you would become lost until you find another teacher. So remember, within the limitations of your own self-respect and rights, the guru's word is the ultimate truth in that instance, because they have been there and done it, and you are merely and humbly asking the way.

According to the Yoga *Tattva Upanishad*, our inner divinity and potential is covered by a veil of ignorance that obscures it, and prevents us from recognising its nature. The goal of personal practice then, is to remove that ignorance and discover the innate, ever-present divinity within. The guru plays a significant role in this, it is his only role in life as a guru. So he must also be well versed not in the subject matter but also in the skills of teaching. In order to be the best he can be, he must adapt and evolve his teaching style to manage different types of people and bring them to a place of light however necessary. With almost 8 billion people on the planet at the time of writing this book, it is no easy task to find enough teaching styles to manage everyone's unique learning style.

Since we learn from our teachers not just by what they say but also by what they do, it is important the guru fully embodies the methods he speaks of. He need not be perfect for he is still just human, but always striving and always dedicated to the processes he teaches. I'm not claiming to be an expert in all of these paths, but I do practise them all and have had the necessary initiations into my practice by the many gurus, coaches and teachers of my life, whom I thank deeply from my heart.

Every person in this world who chooses to be active in achieving something good, has to go through trials and tribulations. It's easy to just sit there and comment on everybody else's work and progress, but what are you doing? So there are always going to be times in an active person's life where they will experience challenges, disagreements and mistakes. We may not always deal with those experiences well, and we can only hope we will learn and grow from them. Their relativity to the present moment and what we consider to be "the future" is simply that of lessons learned. In those lessons we find out things about ourselves that we can work on, which serve far more importance to our overall development than the failings of others around us. Passively observing the external world and noticing the failings of other people is easy. It serves no purpose except petty point-scoring and defaming, from an inexperienced judge who is only really reinforcing their own ideas by criticising another's. There is no learning to be done there, only an echo-chamber. The inward-directed perspective grants us the power to know how we can do better and keep getting better, regardless of what we may inevitably face and therefore cannot control.

Our ability to control thought is free will, and to know which thoughts to act upon is spirituality. I'm not claiming to be non-emotional, to not experience sadness, anger, etc. But I'm able to observe those emotions, without judging myself for feeling them. Learning how to choose the way I act as a result of those emotions, not acting in a way chosen by them. And finally, through continuing practice of self-awareness, discovering why I experience those emotions and healing those aspects of me that produce them. As a result, neither am I claiming to be awakened, enlightened or "woke" – an important note to make is that the famous Buddha Siddharta Gautama's enlightenment was not self-proclaimed, it was the Earth who witnessed his enlightenment. Gautama was seated in meditation and challenged by the demon Mara, who had confronted him and was saying that he is more enlightened than him. Mara raised his demonic army to stand and testify to his power, then asked Gautama who will speak for him. Gautama remained silent and touched the ground with his index finger – the Earth itself roared "I am his witness", and Mara with all his army disappeared. The message seems to tell us that simply living in accordance with natural laws and in harmony with the cosmos leads us to a place where we are acknowledged and sustained by the same.

"Many modern Gurus put far too much emphasis on gaining spiritual experiences, but not enough emphasis on gaining spiritual wisdom. All experiences are temporary, including experiences of enlightenment, or Kundalini. After a powerful spiritual experience comes and goes, you might remain utterly unchanged, unless

you actually learn something from that experience." For this reason, the ultimate goal of spiritual practice is not to produce short-lived experiences, but rather to reveal the true divine nature of the consciousness within."
— **Swami Dayananda**

We are now in what I like to call the "Self-help Age". We are taking back responsibility for self and in that there is great evolution and progress for humanity. As I said before you can be shown the way but you have to walk it yourself. We must work to create order internally, so that we can live with the "chaos" or uncontrollable nature of the herd and the external environment. We are so lucky that the sun rises and sets when it needs to, and that everything else is just happening as it should. We need only learn to control ourselves to come closer to a more harmonious and peaceful way of living this space – make no mistake, we were not put here, we came and grew from here. We are an inseparable part of the environment, for we would die if taken out of it. We must learn to live alongside it and with it.

In my own personal role as a guru in today's society, I put all my heart and energy into teaching not just individuals and athletes but also other coaches and therapists across the world. I have uncovered such depth of information that I want to share the joys of this with others, my mission being to upskill the industry of physical coaching, where my personal talents and passions are most intense. I figured, if I can affect one person by coaching them today face to face, coaching other teachers means I can indirectly affect their client's progress, and thus each coach or therapist initiated into my teachings will pass on those teachings in some format and help spread it to the world. I also need not have the credit for that, since I have never made it compulsory that a student of mine quotes me as their guru – I would deem it a standard course of respect yes, but unfortunately it does not always happen and is not in my control. I do this not for my name, but for the good will and love I have towards the universe, source consciousness (God) and the progress of our entire planet Mother Earth (Gaia).

Biohackers, therapists, scientists and mystics alike have all discovered parts of the puzzle over the ages for the natural development and engineering of the human mind and body. We must teach ourselves and the next generation to be still, move, feel and think better - not just for our comfort or health, but for our advancement as a species, for our future, and for peace.

"You have the tools, you're just distracted." — **Hanane Lazaar**

CHAPTER 7
Birth and Death

न जायते म्रियते वा कदाचि
नायं भूत्वा भविता वा न भूय: |
अजो नित्य: शाश्वतोऽयं पुराणो

न हन्यते हन्यमाने शरीरे || 20 ||

"The soul is neither born, nor does it ever die; nor having once existed, does it ever cease to be. The soul is without birth, eternal, immortal, and ageless. It is not destroyed when the body is destroyed." – **Sri Krishna, Bhagavad Gita**

It's never too late. The sense that there is so much to do and so little time can be intense for anyone. The past has gone and cannot be brought back, living there is a foregone conclusion and hopeless. The future is not here and does not even exist, living there is anxiety. What we must remind ourselves every single day is that there is only here and now, that we can at any moment decide and make the choice to be a different person. To make that something which feels organic and not just like acting, we must do the work to support that manifestation of self.

In addition to the progress we may experience on any path, it's important to note the implications of the ageing body (accumulated material), dysfunctions (accumulated trauma) and karma (accumulated memory).

"Be weary of an old man in a profession where men usually die young."
– Anonymous

I like this quote because of the way it cuts through the stereotype of ageing being synonymous with weakening. It simply states that if there is a type of work or task which creates many young deaths or retirements, you should think twice about what it means to be an old man who is still doing it. It means that this old man has the fortitude, wisdom and inner strength to still be doing it and that he has avoided the common pitfalls which befell those younger casualties, or of those who just gave up. This as well as being able to keep his place amongst a younger, competitive generation, make him a symbol for what dedication, skill and wisdom can give a person.

Age does however bring with it more accumulations of memory or habits if you like, which can be obstructive to our learning and growth. We should be innocently naïve in the sense that we are willing to say that we don't know, yet wise enough to be able to understand whatever is revealed to us. So as we grow physically there is a natural development, maintenance and eventual loss of ability; from the moment we are born as a baby we are picking up imprints from our parents and creating our psychological models of the world. We carry these our entire life, reacting off of these deeply engrained patterns and understandings which are passed down both through subconscious genetic memory and conscious parenting. The child, growing up and beginning to learn a sense of self, explores their own body and the world around them through the 5 senses. Unable to fathom much beyond their own survival, we can only nourish them physically and emotionally to support their development.

By the time they reach adolescence, they are still in a primal state of questioning their existence in the world, many staying like this into adulthood without the appropriate spiritual and emotional nourishment. Nature endows them with the surge of hormones which form the adult physically, yet often the mind and emotion have not come along with it. Is this where we are making most of our mistakes as humanity?
By not sufficiently educating our younger generations in deeper levels of self-inquiry they become only book smart - prime adults of society with the most power in this world yet the least wisdom to use it. Finally, nature reminds and humbles us of the process and the truth by stripping away our flesh, as we become the mature adult. The mature adult, realising impending death, has a change of heart and decides to turn their life around before it's too late. A reform typically happens around

here, having finally learnt through their lessons and regrets. Now elderly, waiting for the final countdown in this lifetime, they decide to refocus their energies onto things that really matter before that happens – those matters of self-awareness, self-love and universal love. Whatever happens there for a person, is the difference between a bitter death and a sweet one.

When considering the average lifespan of a human today (79 years), it has been long held in many traditions that mastering any discipline takes more than one lifetime. As such, lineages were created in order to pass down the knowledge gained previously through genetics (procreation) or teachings (guru-shishya). This brings us to a place where we can understand our individual lives in the context of the Earth's life and the generations of the human race. In 1964, Russian Astrophysicist, Nikolai Kardashev, suggested that civilisations can be categorised based on the amount of energy available to them, creating what is now known as The Kardashev scale shown below.

Kardashev scale:

Type 1 - Planetary civilisation. Can harness the power of its planet. Humans are at around 0.73%.

Type 2 - Stellar civilisation. Can harness the power of its star and solar system. A Dyson sphere (essentially a power plant formed around the sun) powers a Matrioshka brain (an immensely intelligent computer brain).

Type 3 - Galactic civilisation. Can harness the power of its galaxy and all stars/systems within it. "Aliens" from other systems who had this level of technology could space travel.

Type 4 - Can harness the power of multiple galaxies. This could be likened to the power of the ancient demi-gods and deities - those whose names were etched onto rock and stone as legends.

Type 5 - Can harness the power of its universe and parallel galaxies within it. The upper eschelon of consciousness, stronger deities but not invincible.

Type 6 - Has the power to create and destroy multiple universes. Invincible. The strongest of the Gods, on which the existence of this universe depends. The Holy Trinity of nature; Creation, Maintenance, Destruction. God, Jesus and the Holy Spirit. Brahma, Vishnu, Shiva.

Type 7 - The singularity of consciousness, the source of all awakening. Krishna-consciousness, Christ-consciousness, Ar-Rahman.

Writing this book has been especially cathartic for me – being able to release and put down onto paper such broad but interconnected topics has been immensely empowering for my soul. During the drafting stage I was writing and editing for 12 hours a day, the words were just pouring out. Upon completion I got a light feeling, floating on the highs of not just releasing that energy and information which has cycling around inside me but of knowing that this can help people the world over and therefore achieve it's true goal.

Samadhisya Amruta Drave
"In the state of Samadhi, nectar flows."

When we're discussing routes for people to achieve a higher level of perception, I am a believer in the perspective that help should be offered as prescriptions, not restrictions. This leaves the onus and responsibility on the individual to take control of their own destiny and avoids the need for people to have to agree on personal beliefs. A doctor can give you a prescription or advice, perhaps even very strong advice, but you are not required to take it by any law. A preacher however always gives strong advice and you are "required" to take it by their laws, else fall out of favour with the universe. This latter method of giving restrictions to people forces them to make choices based in psychological fear of punishment and judgement, rather than through the self-awareness and respect for natural consequences that prescriptions can offer us.

"Our deepest fear is not that we are inadequate. Our deepest fear is that we are powerful beyond measure. It is our light, not our darkness that most frightens us. We ask ourselves, 'Who am I to be brilliant, gorgeous, talented, fabulous?' Actually, who are you not to be? Your playing small does not serve the world. There is nothing enlightened about shrinking so that other people won't feel insecure around you. We are all meant to shine, as children do. We were born to make manifest the glory that is within us. It's not just in some of us; it's in everyone. And as we let our own light shine, we unconsciously give other people permission to do the same. As we are liberated from our own fear, our presence automatically liberates others."
– Marianne Williamson

"The greatest satisfaction a person can have is the bringing of life into light. So whenever we create antagonisms, we simply deprive ourselves of something. When we perpetuate these feelings, we perpetuate the impoverishment of ourselves. So everywhere where fear, worry, anxiety, doubt, anger, anguish, overambition, frustration, wherever any of these emotions exist, there is an energy crying out to be used constructively. To be put to work. To do something, which makes life better. If you use it that way, someday you will receive the reaction. Something that you have done, will become a great source of internal realisation, of achievement in the name of truth.

The physical body follows the mind and imitates the changes. Every change in thought makes a vibration in your mental body, and this, when transmitted to the physical body, causes activity in the nervous matter of the brain. This activity in the brain and nerve cells causes electrical and chemical changes in the body."
– Yogi Swami Sivananda Saraswati

"What you call 'Me' is the spirit. If your life is about the spirit/soul or consciousness, then we say you're spiritual. If your life is about the body, the mind, and what is around you then we say you're material, because these are all accumulated things. What you accumulate can be yours... but can never ever be you. Your mind and body have been gathered from memories and materials... right now if your life has become just about what you have gathered, then it's not about you. Are you on the surface, or are you moving towards the core?"
– Sadhguru Jaggi Vasudev

"Your senses are outward bound and bring messages into the body, which are then analysed. You can't roll your own eyes inward and look at yourself. You can feel an ant crawl on your skin but you can't feel all that blood pumping around you? When you look at me, where am I? You point at me, but really the light from me is going to your retina and your brain is analysing an internal image. Where is my voice? Within you.

In the same way, everything you sense about the world is first translated into movements of energy and molecules inside you, and then analysed. So everything you think you experience is actually an analysis or internal translation of messages from your senses - everything you experience is within. If you change your perspective you can experience a different world - see it how you want to see it and it will become as such.

Your thoughts have the power to become reality through this same method. What you make of what you absorb through your senses is how you make the world for yourself. Some people take drugs or drink or party or whatever, because they want something more than this. If you just enhance your perception, you will lose the desire for something more - you will see that it is happening in such proportions around you... you have to learn to handle it."
– Sadhguru Jaggi Vasudev

"It is a folly for a man to pray to the gods for that which he has the power to obtain himself." – **Epicurus**

"There are many truths. There is a truth for every being and for every particle of the universe, for each one reflects its Master in a different way. To seek truth means more than finding your own truth. It means finding a truth that works for you and for the other guy, for now and forever, in this place and everywhere, for the body and for the soul, for the sage and for the young, innocent child. The higher the truth, the fewer boundaries it knows." – **Rebbe Menachem M. Schneerson**

"Surrender to the great invisible force that is behind everything. Any other surrender will not suffice to leave this maya (life of illusions). This is the final niyama (observation) of Yoga." – **Patanjali, Yoga Sutras**

We were given the gift of being human. According to modern science there are only 5 beings on Earth which are self-aware. Those are the Elephant, Dolphin, Magpie, Ape family and Humans. This was researched by placing red dots onto the animal's bodies and showing them their own image in a mirror. Through seeing their own image in the mirror and recognising themselves, these particular animals realised that the red dot was on their own bodies, showing that they had an awareness of self. The rest of the animals are not self-aware – they're just living their lives and experiencing everything as nature intends for them. They never ask themselves, "Who am I? What am I?" These 5 self-aware beings including us, humans, can though. And through this self-inquiry comes the truth we are seeking, since it is in us that the key to the universe resides, since we are in and out, a micro-expression of the infinite macrocosm.

In our bodies and minds we have been divided from the eternal and others. This division with the world leads us to desire either the destruction of a broken world to reset, or the reconnection of it to whole again. Each viewpoint wants the same thing, a return to stability and peace. Now usually, that specific desire and viewpoint is where someone would draw their strength from in life. It's their general ethic on the best route for the world to achieve peace. This strong viewpoint and drive in you will manifest itself as your mental, physical and spiritual power. And so every person comes to a point in their life where they stop fighting against everything the world wants them to be and surrenders to everything they were born to be. Change is the essence of life - be willing to surrender what you are for what you could become.

I hope to write my next book soon, which will focus in on the topic, field of study and practice that is Movement; a path which chose me as much as I chose it.

Ode to India

I know there will be alternative and opposing viewpoints to the ones I have presented here. I am not married to these opinions, they are just my current understanding and interpretations. To those people who will quote me out of context, remember all nuanced information has a build-up and an afterthought. For those who might want to pick apart what I'm writing, I'm happy to discuss any of the topics with those who have different opinions, but let's keep it on a high vibration all in the name of progress and truth, otherwise go pick a struggle (meaning decide what challenge you really want to focus your efforts and energies on). I'm only interested in the kind of conversation which can lead us to a better understanding of ourselves, each other and the infinite cosmos - like the motto on the Indian flag, **Satyameva Jayate** – *"The Truth alone Triumphs."*

The ingenuity of the Yogic and Vedic sciences is that through simply following the process you are awakened to a new level of perception where you can start to understand the answers to these questions by your own reasoning. Science is not taught at advanced or existential levels to kids straight away, because those levels of understanding require a much deeper level of self-inquiry. Who am I? What is the cause of this material Universe? The intellect cannot answer these things. Yoga, Breath control, Meditation and Jnana (Knowledge) are Krishna's and Shiva's gifts to humanity, they are the processes by which we may self-inquire and come to know our real selves, which is soul, which is source consciousness. When the Yogi is seated in that state of realisation, he attains Samadhi, the still and infinite bliss of absorption in the cosmic energies, momentarily and willingly cocooned from the transient experiences of the external world. There, he basks in the heaven of his own soul.

Hari Om ॐ

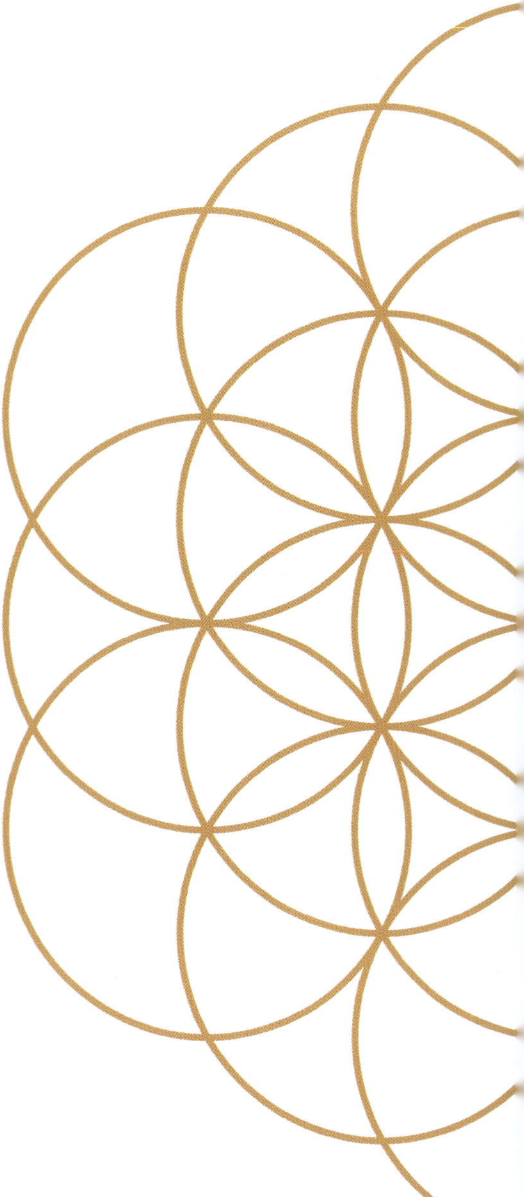

Printed in Great Britain
by Amazon